SHAPING
FOR TOMOR

FUTURE FAITH

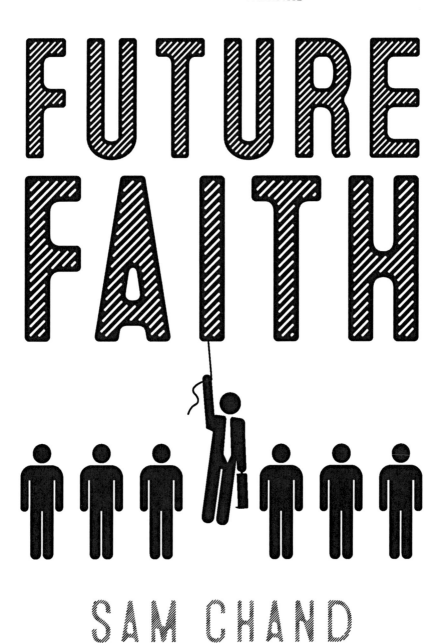

SAM CHAND

FutureFaith:
Shaping Today's Ministry for Tomorrow's Opportunities

by Sam Chand
copyright ©2017

Trade paperback ISBN: 978-1-943294-60-2
Cover design by Vanessa Mendozzi

CONTENTS

ONE

THIS AIN'T YOUR DADDY'S CHURCH

THIS AIN'T YOUR DADDY'S CHURCH!" said one pastor at a conference composed mostly of baby boomers. "The church of yesterday isn't the church of today."

Although that may sound obvious, churches tend to keep on doing things the way they did them a generation ago. Maybe we don't like to hear exhortations to reexamine our methods because we don't like being pushed to alter the way we've always done things.

Change has never been easy. In the late 1920s, many church leaders denounced the use of radio as a medium to present the gospel. Less than thirty years later, they debated the rightness of using television to proclaim the message. Such arguments sound ludicrous to emerging leaders of the future church.

We may not like certain innovations, but we can't get away from movement. If the past teaches us anything, it's that the methods we used a generation ago probably aren't effective now. So where do we, the church, fit into this flux? Do we follow every whim or new idea? Of course not. But we don't stand rigidly firm either. The church is in the business of effectively and relevantly communicating a holistic, life-changing gospel; therefore, we have to adjust our methods to meet the times.

Here's the principle: Our foundational message remains the same. We stand on the fact that "Jesus Christ is the same yesterday and today and forever" (Heb. 13:8). Our methods for presenting the truth not only need to change; they must change.

As the man said: "This ain't your daddy's church!" And I would add, "It's not your granddaddy's either!" Too often church leaders have held on to old methods because they worked in the past with Daddy and Granddaddy. They may not work, however, with baby boomers, busters, and Gen-Xers, or mosaics—as we call the younger generations.

I've used the term *futurefaith* as my way of saying that we need to reexamine the "old-time religion."

We need to separate methods and attitudes from biblical principles. Those of us who commit ourselves to grow and interact with the world around us realize that we need to change our thinking and our perceptions. What worked for Daddy and Granddaddy may be as obsolete as foot warmers in horse-drawn carriages.

Today change happens in the pulpit, in boardrooms, and on the streets. The catalysts are those I call "redefined leaders," people who hold leadership roles in the church. By that term, I refer to four significant characteristics: They (1) look at new paradigms of ministry; (2) are future focused; (3) embrace relevancy as a core issue; and (4) are vision-and-purpose driven. Leadership refers to the pastor surely but just as well to the office staff, Sunday school teachers, ushers, and anyone willing to work in the church.

In this book, my purpose is to

- encourage those in any position of leadership who want to communicate the gospel effectively
- show why and how we must change in the present to prepare for the years ahead
- suggest practical ways to enable us to develop into the future church—the church committed to the eternal gospel that seeks new methods to reach and enrich others
- serve as a catalyst for categories of new thinking

TWO

THE FUTUREFAITH CHURCH

WHAT? WHY? HOW? WHEN?

FOUR QUESTIONS LOOM BEFORE THE church today—*What? Why? How?* and *When?*—and leaders have to answer each of them. Furthermore, they need to know which one to answer first and in what order to answer the others. Too many church leaders respond to the wrong questions and in the wrong order. In so doing, they come up with ineffective answers.

Effective leaders know that two of the four questions take priority. The question leaders choose to answer first tells us much about their attitudes and methods. In this book, I use the term *futuring leaders* to refer to church leaders who have a firm vision of where they want to go in the future. Consequently, futuring leaders first answer What? Then they ask Why?

By answering these two questions first, they begin to define the direction in which the local congregation should go and to form a process to get them headed in that direction. Since their search for answers has a direct relationship to the mission and vision of the institution, they need to define their problem areas. The question What? does exactly that.

"What is the challenge before us?" futuring leaders must first ask. Their question may take various forms, but it will lead them to ask and answer others. Once they discover the solution, they will seek options to implement the what. Once they have decided on what, they are ready to move on to the second question: Why? They need to understand the reason they are taking a particular step. Thus they ask, "Why are we doing this?"

When I asked one pastor why his congregation had chosen to underwrite a particular program, he stared at me for several seconds.

"Everyone knows why," he said. "The answer is obvious even to people who don't know the message of salvation." He spoke to me as if I were a child.

I just smiled. But what if I had answered, "I don't know why." Would he have explained? Or would he have sneered at my stupidity?

Or wasn't I really stupid?

This leads me to ask, Do we have the right to assume that everyone in our church knows why leadership chooses to do a certain thing? I doubt it. For instance, the pastor makes a big push for increased evangelism. From his perspective some of the answers to why would be:

- We can win more people to Jesus Christ.
- We'll have more people in the church.
- We'll have more money to expand our church programs.
- We'll have a greater influence in the community.

His list of why answers may not be the same as that of the congregation he's trying to lead.

By thinking of others' reasons, fears, and needs, futuring leaders can understand the resistance and either rethink their own purposes or find ways to get into others' frames of reference. They also avoid inevitable conflict because they have already prepared for and overcome most of the hindrances.

Once leaders have asked and answered What? and Why? they're ready to move on to the next two questions: How? and When? This second set of questions implies action. It's as if we're saying, "We've made the decision to act. Now we need to figure out how to go about accomplishing our goal and determine when we can implement our plan."

Again, here is where many leaders miss out. They need to be aware that implementing the how and when means change. I like to think of it this way: If we think differently, we'll see differently. How we think shapes the actions we choose.

The greatest challenge facing church leaders is making executive decisions from a variety of different viewpoints. Sometimes we make decisions from the perspective of management or maintenance. At other times we have operated from a fix-it point of view. Rarely have we pulled in all those who will be involved by the changes and said, "You are part of this change in procedure. Your job may be to answer the telephone, but even that is a vital ingredient in this program."

Here's another way to look at the same issue. Let's compare the difference between old leadership styles and new leadership styles, or furturefaith thinking. In the old style—and I refer primarily to the methods used prior to the end of the twentieth century—leaders studied the past and understood the way things operated in 1959 or 1989. When they moved into 2000, they made a few changes—that is, they adapted to what was going on—but mainly they replicated what they and others had done in the past. Because they made a few adaptations, they called that progress.

"What did they do back then?" was the primary question used to help them cope in the present. In contrast to the old style, the new leadership peers into the future, pauses, thinks about the present, and asks:

- What's going to happen in the future?
- How can we position ourselves in the present to be ready to move into the future?
- How can we design a program for what lies ahead?

Futurefaith leaders get their answers by looking at such factors as demographics and economic growth. They use those answers to shape the present and guide them toward the future.

PRESERVING THE PAST OR SHAPING THE FUTURE?

Too often, however, church leaders still caught up in preserving the attitudes and traditions that prevailed thirty years ago don't know how to look at the future. For too long, those in every level of leadership have taken a reactive posture, resulting in attitudes and vision usually lagging about ten years behind industry and technology. Church leaders could move ahead by simply asking: "As a local congregation and as witnesses of Jesus Christ, what are our needs? What are the needs we see around us that we can help to meet? What kinds of needs will we need to meet in the years ahead?"

As we form answers, we need to remind ourselves that most church members live in a highly technological world six days a week. Even in 1997, how many people would have envisioned having their own web site? Yet today numerous congregations have their own web sites. Many people attend a church where song lyrics are displayed on a screen by an overhead projector. Those who sit near the back squint, and if the light isn't right, they can't read the words. They have been using that system for a decade, and it's already out of date. When I preach in larger, forward-looking churches, they have huge screens the size of a wall on either side of the platform on which they project lyrics and often the music. They also project the speaker on those screens so that he or she can be viewed from anywhere in the building.

The sound system microphone used to hang from the ceiling with a long cord just above the pulpit. In progressive churches, microphones are dispersed all over the congregation. Some churches have "seeded" singers with cordless microphones. When the congregation sings, those seeded singers encourage those sitting around them to sing out. As a result, the singing has a more vigorous, exciting sound.

Futurefaith leaders should know this: We need to use technology.

I like to think of the present situation in the church as being much like the use of a remote control. These days most families have that little battery-operated mechanism for running TV, VCR, CD, and DVD players. People have become so accustomed to remotes that even when they leave home, they take mental remotes with them. They're still using those remotes even when they attend church. They stare at the strange building that doesn't look like anything except a church. It has stained-glass windows on the outside, perhaps a bell, and certainly a steeple. Suddenly and unconsciously, "click-click" goes the remote, and they say to themselves, "How does this relate to me? Why should I listen? Is this real life?"

Perhaps they do come inside and sit in a pew—an uncomfortable piece of furniture used nowhere else today except in church buildings. They sit down and listen to pastors who preach the same sermons in content and length that they preached ten years ago.

"This is the answer!" the preachers cry out. "This is the way to [salvation, growth, healing, prosperity, or peace]." They have a number of specific answers to handle each problem that confronts the local congregation, the church at large, and society in general. Unfortunately for those preachers, they haven't figured out that some of those problems aren't so answerable and directions aren't as clear as they once were.

"Click-click" and the remote switches to another mental channel.

FROM THE ABSOLUTE TO THE AMBIGUOUS

We have moved from a world of the absolute to the ambiguous. We're asking ethical questions that people haven't asked before; for example:

- Fifty years ago, how many committed Christians married outside their denomination? Who worries about that today?

- Twenty years ago, how many churches acknowledged that some marriages between believers didn't last until parted by death?

- In Mama's church, how many members seriously debated issues such as euthanasia or sexual reassignment?

- A generation ago, how many Christians expressed concern about the environment, practiced recycling, or questioned whether we would have enough fossil fuels for our grandchildren's generation?

- When I was a boy, I heard Christians scream out against cremation, but who fights that issue today?

Futurefaith leaders have moved from answering questions that nobody asks anymore to discussing the nittygritty issues of life that concern and confuse people. Society has changed; we have lost the stability our parents and grandparents enjoyed and took for granted.

Futuring pastors no longer preach forty-five-minute sermons, because they know the remotes are clicking away, and they would be tuned out before they had preached even thirty minutes. In fact, maybe sermons need to be done in snippets—points interspersed with songs, Bible readings, dramas, and video clips. Someone said we need to think of the modern sermon as "Karaoke preaching," in which the preacher stands in the middle of the congregation like an interactive television talk show host. The futuring church must find new ways of presenting the gospel before they're tuned out by the ever-present mental remotes.

THINKING IN NEW WAYS

To move into the futurefaith mentality, we have to accept one important reality: Most worship services are patterned after practices of a century ago, and those methods no longer attract people to the faith.

Futuring leaders must move into a thinking-leading style of leadership in which they see relationships and possibilities that still elude others. This is the idea I had in mind once when I spoke to a group of pastors. "The greatest challenge is not your location. It is not your finances, and it is not your staff," I said. "The greatest challenge is your thinking. If you can change your way of thinking, you can change everything." I reminded them that we're in a thinking era and we have to question everything. In the past, we continued to do things a certain way because that was the way the leaders before us operated. That plan no longer works.

Futuring leaders question everything.

- "Why are we doing this?"
- "Are we still doing that?"
- "Is that the best way to use our resources?"
- "Is there a better way to do this?"
- "Why is she still doing that?"
- "Is he competent to do this?"

THREE

IMMIGRANTS VS. NATIVES

TWO GROUPS

IN THE PULPITS, SUNDAY SCHOOL classrooms, and every area of church leadership, we make pronouncements—and we often do it with authority. We have historical precedent behind us, we know what we're saying and doing, and we know why. What we don't grasp is that those who receive our messages have a different outlook and divergent values, and the message we send isn't the message they receive.

One way to understand this dilemma is to talk about the two distinct groups of people in almost every congregation—immigrants and natives (terms I borrowed from Leonard Sweet). As you read this, ask yourself, "Am I an immigrant or a native?" If you'll seriously consider the question and its implications, the answer may surprise you. Neither is bad.

Natives, as the term implies, are those who have been in the church—especially in one particular congregation—for a long time. They have been there long enough to know the congregation's history and can speak of the trials and hardships of building the membership through the years. Someone has said that everyone who is forty years old and has been in a church for at least a decade is a native. That age isn't meant literally, but is used only to refer to the general thinking of those in that group. I know some seventy-eight-year-olds who still think young. I also know twenty-five-year-olds who are native in their thinking.

Immigrants, by contrast, come into a church and try to understand the language of a congregation, which is often like a foreign dialect to them. To fit in, they have to tread carefully until they learn the sacred words and symbols. Only then will they be accepted as orthodox believers.

The two groups can be distinguished by contrasting their characteristics.

Natives	Immigrants
Slow deciders	Fast deciders
Threatened by change	Lead change
"Yes . . . but"	"Yes . . . and"
Linear thinking	Looped thinking
Fight against chaos	Can live with chaos, uncertainty, and instability
Learn formally	Learn by discovery—by doing it
Visual—primarily through books	Visual—primarily through TV and media

In some ways, of course, all of us are immigrants even if we are natives within our local church. For example, helping my two daughters with their homework overwhelms me. I can't sit down in the evening and assist them with their math homework the way my parents did with me. In my day, we learned fractions and decimals by a different process than students arrive at them now. Not that one is right and the other is wrong; they simply do their math from another perspective. Consequently, in this case, they're immigrants and I'm a native. To carry this further, when I did homework at home, we had no interference from the radio, TV, tape player, or CD player. We sat at the kitchen table before or after dinner and worked there until we completed our assignments.

Both my daughters amaze me. They can have the TV blaring, talk with a friend on the phone, and type an email message—all while they're doing homework. Their generation is made up of multitaskers while their parents were taught to be one-task people.

Here are a few other contrasts:

- My generation was into permanence and stability, but that's not possible or desirable today.

- We readily accepted whatever authority figures said, but today's youth question authority. They raise eyebrows at authoritative voices or react cynically to once-accepted messages.

- Print was the truth medium. If we read something in a newspaper, and especially if it appeared in book form, it was truth without question. For today's youth, TV is the truth—well, usually.

- When I asked, "Why?" my father would answer, "Just because I said so," and that would end the discussion. That's not the end of the discussion now. In fact, we rarely speak those words to our children.

How does this relate to an organization such as the church? Let's say the pastor is an immigrant—which is likely when first coming to a new congregation. Who greets the immigrant? The natives, of course—and that includes the staff as well as the congregation. How the pastor and natives communicate with one another becomes extremely important. (Of course, some pastors are natives—they may have moved two or three times in their career, but they take the past with them and replicate what they have taught and preached for the previous twenty years.)

Natives are those who perpetuate the past by trying to relive it in the present. Whatever they are doing now or have been doing is the "right thing." This often means that when immigrants attend a church, the teaching natives prescribe books and courses written by natives who learned from other natives.

Immigrants come into the church and hear the same kind of sermons their parents heard in 1975. The church service is still predictable. After they have attended two Sundays, they know how the service will start and when it is going to end. They know what will happen at 11:15 and can guess within sixty seconds when the service will end.

Today many pastors come in as natives—bringing the past with them—and they hire staff members who are mostly immigrants. The new staff people are younger, have been to college since the pastor graduated, and are reading and listening to different things.

In most cases, the congregation—if the church is growing—is composed of natives and an increasing number of immigrants. The immigrants differ from their parents, all the structure is different, and the leadership is still native—in its thinking, attitude, and ways of doing things.

When I start asking natives the why question, they sometimes resent the question itself or act offended as though the query is a criticism. To an immigrant, why is a reasonable thing to ask, because he or she has been taught to raise issues. Immigrants are a questioning people; natives were taught to be an answering people.

What does this mean for the people who want to bring in the immigrants? For one thing, unlike the generation before them, they face the reality that those immigrants aren't searching for leaders who have all the answers. Rather, they seek leaders who raise relevant questions. The most effective leaders sit in a business meeting and ask, "What about_____?" Those leaders know that if they raise the right issues, they can help guide others to the right answers. They don't have to provide all the knowledge, insight, and wisdom, but they do have to point the way.

Activity used to drive our thinking and our ministry. For instance, a Sunday school superintendent would say, "We're going to have backyard Bible clubs all summer." That's an activity, and the clubs were effective—in 1980. That style of thinking has changed. Today if a native says, "We're going to have a backyard Bible club," an immigrant immediately asks, "Why do we want to do that?"

A flustered native sees this questioning as opposition or resistance. The immigrant might then say, "Okay, but why the Smith backyard? Why not at the Hansons across the street or the Randolphs in the next block? What's so strategic about the Smith backyard?" After the native reluctantly gives an answer, another immigrant asks, "What are we going to do with the clubs to follow up?"

Twenty years ago, some natives hadn't ever considered anything beyond holding the club activities, presenting Jesus Christ as the Savior, and informing the congregation of the number of first-time decisions for Jesus Christ. For them, just having and staffing a backyard Bible study was an event. They did their service for the Lord and didn't look ahead.

Today's leaders are saying, "We can no longer be an event-oriented society; we need to move to being a process-driven society." An event is the means and end combined into one. That is, an event begins and ends, while a process focuses primarily on the means, recognizing that the end is usually a mirage. For immigrants, there is only process and no ultimate end in sight. An immigrant is comfortable with the process, whereas natives tend to feel anxious.

Immigrants, for example, think like this. Someone asks, "Why don't we establish places of worship outside the traditional church building?" Actually, this change is already taking place, and it came about because futuring leaders recognized needs, and then they asked and answered the right questions. From there they began activities to respond to those needs.

As a result, some organizations now provide chapels or places of worship at their work sites. Many churches use movie theaters and hotels. Business gurus like Stephen Covey and Ken Blanchard recommend them. Even some airports now have chapels and paid chaplains.

FROM TRANSACTION TO TRANSFORMATION

Immigrants understand that people have needs at pressure points in their lives. They're trying to meet those needs through collaboration and connections rather than depending on one or two churches that try to do everything themselves. It's a matter of cooperating instead of lone-wolfing.

This leads us to another serious question for futuring leaders. They ask, "Who else do I need to make this happen?" If futurefaith leaders strive to find the answer, things not only begin to happen, but immigrants feel that the natives care about them.

No longer can a church say, "Here we are! Come and find out what we believe." Now the futuring churches are asking, "How can we help?" Instead of saying, "There are many homeless, so let's start a new homeless shelter," they're asking, "Why should we start that ministry when there's already a shelter downtown? How can we resource them?" And they're asking, "Why should we start a home for unwed mothers? Let's find out who is already providing that service and then figure out what we can do to enhance their efforts." Or "Why should we clog up our basement with musty clothes when there are places we can take them?"

The question is not "What can we do?" The question is "What can we do through others?" That's a new way of thinking. Rather than asking, "How can I increase my power and influence? How can I enlarge my kingdom?" we should ask, "How can I empower somebody else and still meet my mission?" This kind of thinking is transformational and not just transactional. Transformation happens when there is active collaboration toward the same goals, and then the mission becomes a win-win proposition.

When people move from transaction to transformation, they're reaching into immigrant country. Instead of trying to do everything themselves, they're learning to empower others. Such transformation begins with a readiness to change.

FOUR
CHANGE READINESS

BEGINNING WITH CHANGE READINESS, THE following chapters describe the ten traits of futuring leadership. Change readiness describes the attitude of embracing rather than resisting change. Whenever change comes about, many leaders focus positively on the gains and overlook the fact that many people concentrate on loss. We need to learn to handle both. It is difficult for natives to accept change because they perceive it as giving up.

Those who want to be a vital part of the futuring church must ask themselves two questions: First, what in my thinking needs to change? Second, what keeps me from making those changes? I regularly ask myself these two questions, and the answers I get aren't always pleasant. In my case, I have to loosen the screws. That is, I have to let go of more things, delegate, and surrender control.

As a native and a church leader, I was taught (indirectly) that leaders are always in control. I came to this quite naturally, because my father was a pastor and I became a pastor. And because I loved and respected my father, I emulated him in many ways.

Like other pastors who went through ministerial training when I did, my tendency was to become a control freak. We hate the term, but it's a strong part of most leaders. Although we never admitted to having a need to control or dominate, the need was nonetheless real. Whether consciously or subconsciously, we believed we were the center of the church universe. It was our responsibility to keep everything moving in the "right direction" (translate "right direction" as my way of doing things). If we didn't keep everything within our control, we had failed! When I became president of Beulah Heights Bible College, I transferred that need for control and taking charge. I didn't enlarge my understanding, and I didn't change tactics or attempt new strategies. I went from being a pastor to a college president, but my operating methods stayed the same. That is, they did until I began asking myself those two questions—and demanding answers from myself.

MY ANSWERS

The answers I had to admit to myself came out of much heart searching, deep introspection, and not a small amount of embarrassment.

First, "What in my thinking needs to change?" I needed to realize that I don't have to control every action and every outcome. This isn't a question we answer once and it's over. It's a question that demands frequent internal checkups.

Second, "What keeps me from making those changes?" Sam Chand was the biggest problem, because he didn't change quickly. He understood the principle of futurefaith leadership for several years before he began to learn to live by the principle of surrendering control (a stronger and perhaps more accurate way of saying it is "giving up power"). I still have a little trouble with him in that area, but he is learning.

Most of us have an operating principle we live by, especially when we are thrust into leadership roles. Twenty years ago, we referred to that as our model, and today we use the word paradigm. However we say it, we mean that each of us has a set of internal values and attitudes that determines how we function. My paradigm was that the pastor is in total control and holds the power in the church. Many of us natives grew up with that same model. At its extreme, it means that no one dares to make a single decision unless it bears the pastor's imprint. The pastor becomes the deciding factor and final word on everything that happens in the church.

Part of my growth in the futuring church has been learning to trust others—and it has been a learning process—and encouraging them to express their abilities. At one point, I would have said "allowing them" to express their abilities, indicating that I still held control and was to be viewed as the permission giver. Then I learned that the best use of power is to empower others. We can't fully make the ten traits of futuring church leadership, discussed in the following chapters, realities until we probe deep within ourselves and ask the two questions with which I started this chapter. So before you read on, ask yourself, "Am I ready to change?"

PREPARING FOR CHANGE

Change readiness means we're prepared to embrace change rather than resist it—ready to think new thoughts, adjust our attitudes, and be open to whatever lies ahead of us. It's a mental thing and a spiritual decision. It's also easier to talk about than to make a reality.

We need to remind ourselves that when we alter our attitudes we can produce vast gains. That's the primary reason we advocate change—we readily see the benefits of our decisions. If we [name the activity], then we will [grow, mature, witness more effectively].

We tend to see only the sunshine up ahead and put the "gain spin" on innovative ideas. But change has another side—it also brings about loss. Too often those in leadership don't pause to consider that aspect. Furthermore, those who have to adjust are often ignored. They are the ones who must make the change, which they didn't originate, and they respond in terms of loss. They may say things such as,

- "It won't be the same around here."
- "I used to know everyone by name."
- "I'll feel lost by the sheer size of the building."
- "I liked the music we used to have. Why do we have to keep adding songs that nobody can sing?" (Note that "nobody" refers to those with the same attitudes.)
- "What's wrong with the way we used to do it?"

What these people are really asking is, "What do I have to give up?" and "Why do I have to give in? Why can't others give in?" If they think in such categories and if the losses are too large, leaders will encounter resistance, quiet acquiescence, subtle sabotage, or open rebellion.

In typical church meetings, the leaders talk extensively about what they need to be doing now, but they tend to spend little time discussing what the future holds for them and their congregation's ministry. They talk even less about the implications of change for those who hold leadership positions. Asking, "What needs to happen?" is not as important as asking, "As leaders, what do we need to do?"

Those of us in leadership positions—any leadership position in the church—need to ask, "What am I doing that prevents our ministry from going forward?" We may not like the answers, but we need to hear them anyway. As leaders in any area of ministry, we need to challenge the other members of our committees and boards to consider the future and to be open to change.

One way to go about that is to urge them to reserve in every meeting an agenda item that focuses on the future. "We need to do this in every meeting," we can say as we reserve a place for discussion. We might also prompt dialogue by asking, "What would you like to see happen? What changes would you like to make as we face our future?"

I try to remind people of the world outside our church doors. Think of it this way. Today as I drive down the highway, I see a huge sign indicating that there is a Kroger store to my right. Tomorrow it may not be there. On the third day, a new grocery chain may have moved in. Things change—we all know that. What we haven't fully grasped, however, is how rapidly they change.

Even if we endorse or approve a plan for a new form of ministry, that's not the end. As leaders at every level in the church, we need to ask ourselves, "What is going on with us—individually and as a congregation—that will stop this form of ministry from going forward?"

Sometimes when I make such suggestions, people stare back at me, hardly understanding what I'm trying to say. So usually I give them an example, such as this: Let's say a church is structured so that there are seven elders. What would it be like if each elder had a responsibility to do research as part of that leadership position? One researches the socioeconomic demographics of the community. A second studies the ethnic issues, problems, and opportunities within the community. A third focuses on environmental issues and what the congregation can do to take care of the earth God has given us—especially the part around the church and neighborhood. A fourth investigates the learning and teaching styles in the area schools and explains to Sunday school teachers how they might use those styles to enhance their ministry.

If each of the seven has a research assignment and brings back a report, the church will have some indication of what the future will look like. The church may need to bring in a consultant to pull all the information together and then begin to plan for that future.

Let's say this congregation focuses on the next three years. If they study what is going on now and use the benefit of their research to project what lies ahead, they will function as a futuring church.

For instance, instead of declaring, "This is now a transitional community," they won't have to think in that kind of category, for they would have known three years earlier that it was going to become transitional and change from single housing to apartment housing or that the area was changing from a residential community to a commercial neighborhood. My point is that a futuring church would have acknowledged the transition before it became readily apparent to everyone, and it also would have figured out what it could do about that situation. Too often, however, congregations refuse to acknowledge changes within their communities until after they have taken place and they're forced to see what they didn't want to face.

Instead of finally saying, "All our people have moved," and then hurriedly trying to buy property to move where members of the congregation have relocated, why can't we do transitioning work? For instance, we could say, "It looks as if in three years the Koreans (or Hispanics or African Americans or Caucasians) will be the majority in this area. Should we start now to reach out to them as they come in? Can we integrate? Do we want to integrate? If we choose not to integrate other cultural and ethnic groups, what can we do to bring about a smooth transition rather than a knee-jerk reaction when we have to face the truth that we should have known three years earlier?"

MIND TRANSITION

An even stronger reason for future thinking is that people need time to work through emotional and ethical issues. Wise leaders provide people with time to transition their minds.

None of us just presses mental buttons; we have to adjust our thinking and learn to see from a different perspective.

"What will the future look like?" is a question we in positions of authority need to think through carefully. We need to help those who work under us and with us understand that we can't function effectively with the methods and mind-set of the past.

As I wrote that last statement, it made me wonder how many people in America resisted the automobile. How many refused to buy TV dinners and cake mixes forty years ago? As late as 1999, several of my friends said, "You'll never catch me walking around in public with one of those cell phones." Obviously, people do change their minds, and that alters their behavior. Today I can see some of those once-resistant friends talking on their cell phones as they walk across the church parking lot or through the mall.

My point is that we can't expect most people to make abrupt paradigm changes. We need to remind ourselves that we're not trying to adjust and alter just so we can say, "See, we're different." Our changes need to have a purpose for us to revise our thinking. The major purpose for us as futurefaith people is to become more effective witnesses of Jesus Christ.

This concept reminds me of something J. G. Harlan said: "God gives every bird his food, but he does not throw it into the nest." He meant that opportunities come to those who are prepared to receive them. That's another way to speak of change readiness. What I perceive as an opportunity may be part of God's process in my life. If we're prepared today, God can entrust more opportunities to us.

We have to ask ourselves, "What did I do today to ready myself for the future? Is yesterday's preparation going to carry me through tomorrow? Is there some new preparation I need to make today to carry me through tomorrow?"

Another part of change readiness is accepting and adapting to change. That's difficult for natives, because they have to start with unlearning. In order to embrace change, they must first unlearn some of their ways of doing things.

That takes us back to the two questions. First, what in my thinking needs to change? Second, what keeps me from making those changes? Natives have been taught to look backward, and now we're saying, "No, you can't do that anymore." Thus, some see the futuring church only in terms of having to give up or of having something taken from them. That's the position some natives choose to take (and it is a choice), because it is difficult to adjust and to change thinking habits.

The most difficult thing for me in thinking with an immigrant mind has been and continues to be the unlearning of old patterns of thinking and outdated forms of behavior. I've had to learn to relate to people who have no idea who Hezekiah was or who haven't figured out whether Hebrews is in the Old or New Testament. We used to be able to speak about such things as the mercy seat, being covered with the blood, being sanctified, or carnal behavior. If I use any of those terms in conversation with immigrants, they look at me as if I'm speaking to them in a foreign language.

Futuring churches have found excellent ways to reach out to their communities. Counseling programs have been excellent outreach tools, but many churches have discovered that in-house counseling has more liabilities than assets.

- This is especially true if the senior pastor gets involved.

- If the pastor preaches and also does counseling, some of the listeners assume they are the people the pastor is talking about in his illustrations.

- To overcome this criticism, the preacher avoids using what could be meaningful illustrations. Thus, counseling then disempowers the preaching.

Another factor that many congregations have recognized is that the people they help the most in counseling rarely become transformed into the most loyal or faithful. That is, setting up counseling services does not assure an increase in attendance at that church. They may, in fact, be recruiting members for another congregation. Research has shown that those who have received counseling may be embarrassed or have other reasons for not joining the church that helped them. They may, however, make their way to another church and become active.

Many futuring churches have studied the need for counseling and agreed that people need such services, so their answer is to outsource counseling. Some contract with counseling services or individual professionals to set up appointments on the church site. Most of the time, those who use the counseling services pay for them but not always. Sometimes a local congregation offers services free or for greatly reduced rates so that more people can take advantage of the therapeutic sessions.

The largest Christian counseling service in the world is called Alpha Care, which is also insurance approved. By hooking up with them or a similar group, churches can provide counseling by outsourcing it to organizations they trust. This arrangement doesn't tie up their staff, somebody else can profit financially, the church and its members are still being serviced, and liabilities are reduced. Doesn't that sound like futuring faith practices at work?

PROMOTING CHANGE

Leaders promote change through thought, word, and action. In the old days, pastors did everything, including promotion. They announced events from the pulpit and promoted the events they wanted to succeed. Their verbal signature was a signal to church members that said, "This is something you should attend."

We now have many subgroups within the congregation, and each of them needs intentional promoters. No single program can or is intended to appeal to every member. That may sound obvious, but when I was a boy, many churches expected all the faithful members to attend every event; even eighty-year-olds were expected at youth activities. They sat unobtrusively (or so they assumed) in the back during youth services. We learned that if we wanted to be counted among the spiritual, we needed to be present at every activity.

How should promotion within the church work today? Let's say that the pastor and a few deacons believe the congregation should relocate. How should they promote this idea? The most obvious place to start is for the pastor to use pulpit time to advocate moving, and that's how they did it in Daddy's church. But today that's not enough.

Advocacy needs to be done through written media, and just as important, announcements need to be made by promoters within subgroups. Promoters must be strategically selected to deal with the core group, with immigrants, and with natives. That is, they should have leadership among every group and subgroup within the congregation.

LEADING CHANGE

When I was thinking about leading change, I scribbled these words:

- Swallow hard and determine to overcome personal reservations of perceived inadequacy and lack of preparation.
- Get out in front and lead.
- If we are going to have change, leaders must be in front of the parade so the crowd knows whom to follow.

"If everything in the world is in transition, why are we—the church—so slow to change?" someone asked. "We only want to change to a sure thing," I said flippantly. The more I thought about it, however, the more I realized how true my words were.

Change involves risk. For instance, if I'm the CEO of a company and I lead the corporation in change and it works, I'm rewarded with high stock options and a large bonus. If, however, the change sends our stocks downward and profits decrease, I'm out of there and no one remembers my name. And it will be a long time before somebody else gives me a chance to lead a growing organization.

In the church, we tend to be conservative—and a little fearful. We want a sure thing before we make our moves. We want a reasonable guarantee of success. However, in the chaos in which we live, there's never going to be a time when we can make a decision with all the data available. By the time we collect enough data to inform us fully so that we can make a decision, the data has already changed. Because we live in this state of constant flux, change leaders have to move from "change" to "churn." By that, I mean that change is an event, such as moving from point A to point B. Churn means we are constantly caught up in chaos. We're continually making adaptations and corrections to the situation.

Timing is important. No longer is there something called "The Plan." Change implementers know the next step, and they probably have a strong concept about the step after that. Some might even be able to foresee step three. After each step, however, they may need to balance everything again. Staff members hired last year may not be the visionaries to take the congregation to the next level of achievement. Deacons elected five years ago may be dragging their feet and holding back the entire congregation. Leading change is difficult. Change leaders must be sensitive and tough at the same time.

I like to look at this concept in terms of a helium balloon. If I am standing inside a building and release a helium-filled balloon from my hand, the balloon will float upward and stop when it touches the ceiling.

Does the balloon have the capacity to go higher? Yes.

What holds the balloon down? The ceiling.

If I want that balloon to rise higher, I have to find a way to raise the ceiling.

Senior pastors are that ceiling, and no congregation can grow beyond the pastor's level of leadership. If the pastor's spiritual growth and leadership skills are stunted by neglect, the church's spiritual and numerical growth will be stunted as well. Senior ministers tend to hire a larger staff and send the newer personnel to conferences and seminars and insist they read books, listen to tapes, and watch videos. The senior pastors, of course, are too busy "doing ministry."

Conductors cannot conduct their orchestra without turning their backs on the crowd. It's not always easy for futuring leaders to turn their backs on the crowd. It is, however, the right thing to do. I would like to ask senior pastors these questions:

1. When was the last time you attended a conference for yourself? I'm not referring to the last time you were the keynote speaker, but the time you went to learn and absorb for yourself.

2. What was the last good book you read?

3. When was the last time you read a book?

4. When was the last time you asked tough questions of yourself about change and growth?

5. When was the last time you asked yourself, "What thinking do I need to change?"

6. What is there about me that is hindering the growth of our congregation?

If leaders ask themselves these questions, they can raise the ceiling. For some, the possibilities may be exciting, but for others, the risks seem too great, so the ceiling stays put.

Leading change requires someone to stand at the front to challenge and cheer on others. Leaders are the risk-takers, and they can make life within the congregation challenging and exciting. They lead in change when they themselves begin to grow. If leaders refuse to grow or neglect personal growth, what kind of example are they setting for members of the church?

In summary, change readiness means that leaders must

1. Prepare for change.

2. Promote change.

3. Lead change.

FIVE

EXPECTING THE UNEXPECTED

THE SECOND TRAIT OF FUTURING leadership is adaptability. Futuring churches expect the unexpected. They go with the flow around them and continue to redirect their course. They recognize that everything around them is changing and will continue to change.

Nevertheless, the church must adapt to the needs of the real world without forsaking biblical standards. Proponents of alternative lifestyles and other moral issues are challenging the church. Although adaptability doesn't mean moving away from God's mandates, we do need to understand those who don't heed the biblical lifestyle.

Immigrants are coming into the church bringing their own values and needs. How do we preach to them? The answer may not be as simple as we think. For example, typically when we preach about the family, we think of the nuclear family—one mother, one father, and children—and we accept that as the norm. But that's no longer the family. Today if a family has two parents, it is most likely a blended family; that is one or both of the parents was previously married and has children from the former marriage. Single-parent families are also on the rise. The 1960 norm is no longer the norm of this millennium.

Another example of change is what is referred to as the graying of America. As a nation, the United States is aging. More people over sixty-five are now alive than at any other time in our history. Each Sunday most pastors preach to three or four generations in the same service.

Such facts mean we must adapt our services and our outreach. The activities we once offered as means of socialization must also change. While we must minister to the graying on one hand, we also have to deal with the fact that 40 percent of the world's population today is under the age of nineteen. Thus, our churches are challenged to reach both ends of the age spectrum. Too many preachers think they can preach one message— that it's still a one-size-fits-all world—and connect with everyone. "This is God's Word," they say defensively. "I proclaim the truth, and God gives the increase."

The purpose of this book is to show the inaccuracy and obsolescence of that mind-set. We who want to lead the futuring church have to learn new styles of leadership, new management techniques, and new technology. Most of us know the language of the natives; now we need to learn the language of the immigrants.

We need to factor in adaptability to changing circumstances. Not only is change coming faster, but it's also coming more frequently and from directions we had not foreseen. In 1970 who would have believed that the biggest agenda item for the church in the first decade of the next millennium would be the issue of sexuality, especially homosexuality?

Who would have imagined that it would have taken Southern Baptists years to decide whether they wanted to keep or oust two congregations that openly accepted homosexuals? In 1995 no one would have believed that they would have considered appointing a committee to study the issue.

"Why would we need to do that?" a native would ask. "We know what's right and we certainly know what's wrong."

NATIVES ARE CERTAIN; IMMIGRANTS AREN'T POSITIVE

We who believe God's Word and know that any kind of sexual behavior condemned in the Bible is sinful also need to understand that our burden is to find ways—kind and caring ways—to extend the gospel to those most in need as we expect the unexpected.

The Southern Baptists ousted those two churches, and that wasn't the surprise. The surprise was that they did so only after much debate and after they had conducted a study. This illustrates the principle of expecting the unexpected.

Years ago we saw the rise in couples living together outside of marriage. We expressed disdain by using derogatory terms for such relationships, including "shacking up." Today the acceptable term is "cohabitation before marriage" and few people blink over the idea. In the past, couples consummated their relationships discreetly, and we assumed they would eventually marry. Today we're seeing more of what I call pre-cohabiting. Couples are sexually active in a monogamous relationship, but the woman has her place and the man has his. Today the woman asks, "Why do I want to give up my home to move in with him? If this relationship doesn't work, I will have lost my home." So now they both keep their homes.

It used to be that as soon as the word expecting or pregnant entered a couple's vocabulary, they hurried to get married. Today expectant couples often delay getting married or don't marry. Some women are choosing to raise their babies on their own. They say, "He'll be involved because he's the father, but he won't be involved as my husband." Natives shudder at such a scenario; immigrants know that's part of the real world. Today we expect the unexpected.

I know of a lesbian relationship in which one of the women conceived a child through artificial insemination. The two women now have a baby daughter, and they want to bring her up "in a Christian church atmosphere." What do we tell them if they come to our church? We need to expect the unexpected.

We used to think of AIDS as a disease that only gays and drug addicts contracted—and only those outside the realm of the church. That's changed; AIDS has now come to church. Many of us began to see it when wives of infected drug users and their babies were diagnosed with the disease.

When those with AIDS do come to church, how do we treat them? Some badly misinformed people still think the disease can be contracted by eating with the same fork or touching the same plate or glass an infected person used. How does the church cope with that? Do we provide separate plates and silverware? How and where do we seat HIV-positive people in our worship services? Do we openly tell people about their situation?

EXPECT THE UNEXPECTED.

Once natives learn that another native or an immigrant has AIDS, what happens during times of informal fellowship? Do we hug them? How do mothers feel about that AIDS-infected person who is a gifted teacher of junior kids? Will they allow their children to attend class? Do parents need to know that their child's teacher has AIDS? What kind of disclosure rights or policy does the church have? Must the church tell the parents? If so, where does that leave the infected person? What about his or her right to privacy?

SHIFTED THINKING

Every day we are being called on to redirect our course without losing our scriptural moorings and forward momentum. How do we do that? Not easily.

I like to think of this as a high-wire act in which we constantly make adjustments as we step across the thin wire. Unfortunately for us in the church, there isn't a straight line to follow from point A to point B. We're not even sure where we're going, and we find ourselves zigging and zagging just to keep our balance. As new constructs come up, we're forced to think in new ways. No longer do we think linearly; now we use "looped" thinking, which means that we process numerous complex ideas at a time.

Consider, for instance, the shift we have to make in our thinking concerning the appropriate time for worship. Among futuring churches, 11:00 Sunday morning is no longer the sacred hour of the week. They say, "We can make any hour sacred." There was a time when churches filled their auditoriums or sanctuaries to capacity at 11:00 then added a second service at 8:30. Some churches even scheduled three or more worship services on Sunday. As I travel around the country and address churches and leaders, I'm seeing an enormous shift from that mentality. I've observed a variety of subgroups, and with the subgroups different needs are being met. Some people may attend the 8:30 service because it is highly liturgical, replete with robes, organ music, and traditional hymns. At the 11:00 service, a band is playing, no one wears robes, and no one opens a hymnal.

Most of the time, young families attend the earliest service. They want to get worship out of the way—not because they're sacrilegious or less devoted, but because they have so many things going on. Yet they do want to start Sunday with their family in church. Leith Anderson points out in his book *Dying for Change* (Bethany, 1990) that 11:00 became the hour of worship when America was a rural, agrarian nation. By that hour, family members could finish their morning chores, hook up their horse to pull the wagon, and arrive at the church down the road. Every Sunday they would spend several hours with their friends and return home just in time to do the evening chores. We haven't been an agrarian or rural culture for at least two generations, yet many churches have fastened on to that nineteenth-century mind-set. Today, however, many service times are changing to reflect the demographics of our communities.

We've learned that we can do everything on Friday night that we do on Sunday mornings. In fact, we can do it on any day of the week and in a more relaxed atmosphere. We're also learning that midweek services are more for development and teaching than they used to be. When I was a boy, Wednesday night was just another devotional type of service. If we attended regularly, everyone counted us among the faithful.

Many growing churches no longer have Sunday school. That fact shocks natives. They probably don't know that Sunday school hasn't always been part of Sunday worship. In the late eighteenth century, Robert Raikes developed the idea of Sunday school because of children who worked in factories. It was their day off, and he wanted to teach them to read and write. It's hard to believe now, but the clergy were some of his biggest opponents.

Some immigrant-thinking churches say that Sunday school has outlived its usefulness. Instead, they offer one experience on Sunday and a different one in the middle of the week. These different experiences encompass the full spectrum of needs—from the youngest children to the youth—that is, they are trying to reach every member of each family regardless of the structure of that family unit. Many of these churches also serve dinner before the activities.

Futurefaith leaders have capitalized on the reality that not everyone works from 9:00 to 5:00. Not only do some people work odd shifts, but some, like a friend of mine, work for ten hours a day for four days, have three days off, and then start their week again. Mail carriers work six days and then have the next two days off. In both of these examples, the days off constantly change. Futuring churches plan various events at different times of the day as well as on different days of the week to meet a variety of needs.

In the mornings, futuring churches usually attract stay-at-home moms and mothers with young children. In the afternoons, say from 3:00 to 5:00, congregations can meet the needs of single adults—especially those who are between jobs. They can also stretch out their hands toward those who won't go to work until later and to those who have just left the office or factory for the day. These examples illustrate that future-thinking congregations no longer devote all their energies to the sacredness of the Sunday morning hour.

HOME CHURCHES

On the other hand, a core of people will attend their home church on Sunday morning, regardless of what happens during the week. They're the people who are usually present three out of any four Sundays in a month. But many immigrants are not familiar with the home church concept. In expecting the unexpected, futuring leaders may find it helpful to think of them as consumers. They take from each church the things that meet their needs.

Today people are shoppers for their faith. They'll come in, check the facilities, compare the services, and see if that church has something they need. If so, they "buy" by worshiping or serving or simply by staying for that service. Just because they bought something from one church doesn't mean they don't comparison shop.

FUTURE FAITH

Futuring leaders know they must be ready to change, and then they adapt to change. There are still eight more qualities they need to embody.

SIX
SENSITIVE ISSUES

THE THIRD TRAIT OF FUTURING LEADERSHIP is sensitivity— being open and compassionate to everyone. This is a difficult concept for natives to grasp, because many of them have operated for years with a particular set of values (often more cultural than biblical). Too often the response to virtually every question was "The Bible says. . . ." When the Bible doesn't specifically address an issue, many Christians retreat to conservative, cultural attitudes. This isn't to condemn anyone—I grew up among the natives—but it is to say that natives tend to live in a world where the colors are black and white with only the slightest hint of gray. Many immigrants look at the same world, and gray dominates everything.

In the old way of doing things, we drew the lines, set the standards, and decided (tacitly if not actually verbally) the norm for membership in our church. If we're going to stretch into future growth, that's no longer possible. We will be pushed to rethink our biblical foundation, and we may have to smash cultural prejudices.

As we of the futuring church move into the realm of greater sensitivity, we will need to focus on three different kinds of issues—cultural, gender, and generational.

CULTURAL ISSUES

The first area that requires our sensitivity is cultural issues. As I implied above, we can no longer make the kind of dogmatic statements that were used in the past. For instance, there was a time in the history of the church when pastors asserted, "If a woman comes to church without her head covered, she is sinning against God." A few months ago I ran into a diatribe written in the 1920s called *Bobbed Hair, Bossy Wives, and Women Preachers*. The title tells us exactly what the author, John R. Rice, had in mind as the normative attitude. In his day and among the native churchgoers, not many people disputed what he had to say.

Cultural sensitivity, however, is more than not being what we were forty or eighty years ago. Cultural sensitivity celebrates differences. It's no longer "us" versus "them." This lack of cultural sensitivity (even appreciation) is one of the great impediments to the growth of any congregation, no matter what the size, the language, or the country. As long as we think of "those people" and "us," we're impeding the advance of God's kingdom. In fact, this is probably the greatest impediment to assimilation that leads to healthy growth.

Cultural sensitivity isn't merely about Koreans, Latinos, African Americans, and Caucasians all worshiping in the same room, although that may be the most conspicuous example. I'm referring to different socioeconomic cultures, such as blue-collar workers and professionals. Mix cultural differences with various educational backgrounds, blend in the social culture, and then add the ethnic background. Is it any wonder we've awakened to diversity in our churches?

Here are two other ways to see this.

Humor. Pastors and other church leaders need to understand that what once seemed funny may not be a harmless joke today. We don't tell stories about the Polish, the Irish, or Mexicans. A few insensitive people still take on an accent, speak condescendingly, and assume they're funny. Some church leaders still tell jokes that put down marriage—the very sacred rite they yearn to protect.

Homecoming events. In the past, many churches celebrated the birth of their congregations by bringing food and having dinner on the grounds. But if we're culturally and racially diverse, how do we make Filipinos, Latinos, and Vietnamese feel part of that celebration? How do we build cultural bridges for everyone to cross over?

GENDER ISSUES

The second area that requires sensitivity is gender issues. I believe that the gifts and callings of God are gender inclusive and not gender exclusive. I realize that there are still many who oppose my point of view. I can accept them and their position, and I hope they can accept me and mine. My position is that God calls a person to ministry, and it has nothing to do with that person's gender. In some roles, however, one gender or the other may be more efficient.

There are always exceptions, but generally speaking— and much of this may come from our cultural background and teaching—men and women think differently. If that's true, they also tend to lead differently.

- Men tend to lead by position, and women tend to lead by relationships.

- Men tend to exercise knowledge; women tend to rely on intuition.

- Men tend to focus on getting the job done; women tend to focus on involving everyone—being more inclusive and more relational.

- Men may want to fix the problem, while women may be very good at hearing, sympathizing, and empathizing.
- Men may want issues to be clear-cut, but many women can see deeper implications.

What role should gender play in the way positions are filled at church? Suppose we need another helper in the nursery. Do we say, "We need a woman to assist in the nursery?" Men can be good fathers and caregivers, can't they? So why must we make the invitation gender specific? Isn't it a bit insulting and archaic to say "male nurse," "female lawyer," or "male flight attendant"?

On the matter of gender sensitivity, futuring church leaders open up and explore possibilities. They are not locked into selecting a specific gender for specific tasks. They are more interested in function and ability than gender.

GENERATIONAL ISSUES

The third area in which futuring leaders must be sensitive is the generational gap.

The term generational gap has been redefined. We have more generations in our church now than we did ten years ago. Thus, we have to ask, "How will the structure, ministry, and leadership be able to meet the needs of all those generations?"

Futuring leaders continue to grow. They become aware of their need to change, they adapt by expecting the unexpected, and they become sensitive to the issues they face—and some of those are situations they've never wrestled with before. They then have to figure out how to express their new understandings.

Futuring leaders continue to grow by staying aware of emerging sensitive issues. This sensitivity enables them to change, to adapt to the future by expecting the unexpected at a deeper level, especially as they venture into territories yet to be explored.

SEVEN

COMMUNICATION TODAY

T HE FOURTH TRAIT OF FUTURING LEADERS is effective communication. For our communication to be effective today, it must cut across generations, cultures, and even across the globe. The biggest dilemma in communication is that each generation communicates and reacts to communication differently—and too often communicators don't realize that their words have gone past their intended receivers.

GENERATIONAL COMMUNICATION

Perhaps the easiest way to explain the problems of generational communication is to use the terms sociologists use to distinguish the generations—seniors, builders, boomers, busters, and mosaics.

LEADERSHIP AND FIVE GENERATIONS

1. Seniors refers to anyone born before 1928. Some place them before 1930. The exact year of birth of people in these categories isn't the issue as much as their socialization and general

attitudes. The socialization of seniors focused on the Great Depression, Franklin Roosevelt's administration, and World War II. They grew up during a time of relative unity in the nation and with a common core of values. With few exceptions, they are the retired generation. Because of the Great Depression experience, many worry about whether they will have enough money to pay their medical bills and sometimes fear that Social Security and Medicare will fail them.

2. Builders refers to the next generation, who came just before the baby boomers. Many of them remember World War II, and all of them can talk about the Korean Conflict. They liked Ike for president and remember the day John Kennedy died. That is, they were born anywhere between the late 1920s and 1945. Builders say, "Be grateful you have a job." They're less concerned about what they do or how fulfilling it may be and more concerned with having work and a paycheck. "Just endure if you don't like what you're doing."

3. Boomers (or baby boomers) are those born between 1946 and 1964. Their attitude is likely to be, "You owe me a job. Give me a good one." These are the offspring of the two older generations. They grew up with Elvis and the Beatles. Most of them had strong feelings about the Vietnam War, which added words such as Agent Orange and Post-Traumatic Stress Disorder (PTSD) to the nation's vocabulary. Their parents had worked to give them a better life, and they learned to expect higher standards of living. Instead of buying small houses and older cars, they say, "I deserve to have the best now."

4. Busters (or Gen-X), those born approximately between 1965 and 1983, say, "Ignore them." This generation of more than 40 million is the offspring of the baby boomers, a population of 77 million Americans. They tend to be serious about life and therefore give consideration to critical decisions. They are also stressed out. School, family, peer pressure, sexuality, techno-stress, finances, high crime, and even political correctness contribute to their stressful lives. Yet they aren't

driven toward success as much as their predecessors. They are self-reliant, believing they can make sense out of their religious faith. This doesn't mean they focus on Christianity; rather, they tend toward a broader view of "spirituality." And at the same time, they're skeptical—which may be a defense against disappointment.

5. Mosaics (or Nexters), born between 1984 and 2002, are well acquainted with technology and are looking for ways to use it. Their attitude toward work moves from mastering tasks, to making money with their skills, to using that money. Until the destruction of the World Trade Center in 2001, Desert Storm was the only American military involvement they personally experienced. They're labeled mosaics because of their eclectic lifestyle, their nonlinear thinking, the fluidity of their personal relationships, and what someone has called their "hybrid spiritual perspective." They baffle their elders by their comfort with contradictions related to everything from spirituality to morality to families and politics. They will enthusiastically pursue spiritual goals, but they are less likely to feel constrained by traditional theological parameters. They are also the most information-overloaded generation.

A large number of this generation saw their parents lose their jobs due to downsizing. Thus, they distrust institutions. They are also the first generation to be socially active since the 1960s. They bring their socially conscious values to the workplace.

GENERATIONAL CULTURES

This five-generation span also reflects the speed of communication. E-mail is both a terrific blessing and a horrible curse. It's terrific because it has accelerated communication; but it's terrible because it has accelerated miscommunication and misinformation. What used to take a week to travel around the globe now can be spread within hours—long before the accuracy of the content has been verified.

I've discovered several web sites devoted just to listing hoaxes and bogus virus threats, often called urban legends. Too many people spread the message without looking at such web sites, and some probably don't even know they exist. Too often they operate out of panic and perpetuate rumors and encourage fear.

Another less obvious but dangerous problem with email is that it can be responsible for the increase of conflict. When we did more snail-mailing, people tended to take time to think through what they wanted to say before they put paper in their typewriter or got out their stationery. Today it's easy to read an e-mail, react, and dash off an answer. In many cases, the immediate response creates conflict because of hurried reading or frenzied responding.

If someone comes to my office, sits down across from my desk, and says, "I disagree with you, Sam," I can begin to deal with that difference. I hear the voice and observe the body language. This is true for all of us, because we interact and involve ourselves with more than just the words. E-mail, however, doesn't give us that luxury. We may automatically dash off a response— and then have to send a series of e-mails to correct our miscommunication.

E-mailing affects the church in many ways. Who is sending out the information? Does it come from an authorized "server"? Can everyone send whatever emails they want to the entire membership? Is it all right for the entire congregation to receive messages from a member who has access to their e-mail addresses and uses that to spread information? What happens if the message sent, even from an authorized person, is misunderstood or misinterpreted? I assure you, this does happen—all the time.

Intra-office communication is another problem area. Suppose a deacon comes into the church kitchen and sees two frying pans left in the wrong place. Maybe there's a Coke can left in a window. The angry deacon fires a heated note by intra-office memo. The receiver gets the memo, reads it hurriedly, and bumps back a response. "They are only teens. Be thankful the place is as clean as it is." Instead of such trivial issues (and such things do happen) being worked out between leadership and the person(s) responsible, they end up spreading among people who don't need to be involved.

During my years of being a pastor, irate church members had two major means of complaint without a face-to-face confrontation. Some chose to use the telephone, and most of the time they were willing to listen for an explanation. Others who wouldn't express strong negative feelings directly chose to write angry letters that came to me via snail mail. Occasionally they pushed envelopes under my door when they came to a church meeting. Most of the time, however, it took at least twenty-four hours before I received and read their angry messages. Sometimes their letters hurt, shocked, or disappointed me. I was surprised that these people would react in such petty ways—and for such trivial reasons. The one advantage I had was time. The delay gave me the opportunity to reflect on what I read, and I was able to think about their needs and concerns. I also had choices on how to respond. I could send back a letter, and that might take as long as three more days, or I could wait a few hours and call the person on the phone. The passing of time can often have a significant healing effect. When I did get back to an irate member, hours or days had passed and the person's anger had usually cooled.

Today the complaints come faster, almost instantaneously. For those unwilling or unable to express anger directly, e-mail is the method. They dash off a few sentences and click the send button. The speed with which these complaints and rapid-fire responses are sent increases the possibility of anger intensifying. My point is that we have changed from a culture that moves slowly to one that is nearly instant. This lays a heavy burden on us to communicate thoughtfully and clearly. I urge people to pause and reflect before typing out a hurried message. In fact, the more urgent I feel about a message, the more slowly I need to respond. Before I press the send button, it helps to ask, "How will he (or she) respond to this e-mail?"

Too many people forget the common rules of kindness and consideration when they pound out their e-mails. Perhaps before we send the next e-mail or intra-office communication either in anger or in response to anger, it may help to think of these words spoken by Jesus:

> "Love your enemies! Pray for those who persecute you! In that way, you will be acting as true children of your Father in heaven. . . . If you love only those who love you, what good is that? Even corrupt tax collectors do that much. If you are kind only to your friends, how are you different from anyone else? Even pagans do that" (Matthew 5:44–47 NLT).

COMMUNICATION ACROSS CULTURES

Anyone who has traveled in other countries knows that we have gestures and speech patterns that are not universally understood. For instance, Americans gesture "OK" by forming a circle with the thumb and index finger, but in South America, that is an obscene gesture. We think nothing of accepting gifts or doing actions with our right hand or our left, because in the United States, there is no difference. In some cultures, however, it is an insult to offer or receive with the left hand.

Words also have different meanings. For instance, the term for a female dog seems to be offensive only in America, but some of our harmless words cause offense in other cultures. In England some consider bloody as a vulgar expression.

EIGHT

TECHNOPHILIA VS. TECHNOPHOBIA

T HE FIFTH CHARACTERISTIC OF FUTURING leaders is that they are not only aware of emerging technology, but they also quickly adopt its use. In this chapter I discuss three types of technology:

1. Information technology.
2. Industrial technology.
3. Business technology.

(Churches, of course, primarily use informational technology.)

Technophilia is the term I use to refer to friendliness and openness to technology. Long gone are the days when anyone argued over whether to adapt to the electronic world. The war is over, and technology won. Our question is: What do we do with technology in the church?

Churches in general have been slow to embrace technology, but futuring leaders urge us to recognize that technology makes information available to us that we didn't have before. As they say in the business world, "Information is power."

Technology provides us with tools we can use to reach people for and teach people about Jesus Christ.

INFORMATIONAL TECHNOLOGY

In the past, we church leaders received most of our information from denominational headquarters, or if we belonged to an independent church, we had a loose-knit network from which we received information formally and informally. In any case, our information sources were fairly limited. Because "this ain't our daddy's church anymore," futurefaith leaders urge us to expand our information sources.

INDUSTRIAL TECHNOLOGY

Perceptive pastors are now asking themselves three questions:

1. What technology do we have right now?
2. What technology do we have right now that needs improving?
3. What new technology can enhance what we're already doing?

Consider, for example, the microphone, which is standard in just about any church today. How can we improve that? We can use hand-held wireless mics. How can we improve that? We can use lavaliere mikes or headsets. These are the kinds of questions a leader has to continually ask. Moreover, we should also reexamine the sound system, the taping system, and the video system. We use industrial technology in an industrial world. This is ministry, of course, and we need little to remind us of that. Nevertheless, it's also industry—and even if we don't like it, we function that way. Thus, we must harness any technology that will enhance our ministry.

BUSINESS TECHNOLOGY

How do we conduct the business of the church? How do we transmit information? We need to find out what kinds of business software will make our churches run more efficiently. What accounting software is available for churches? How can members receive their contribution receipts before January 31 and know they're accurate? How can pastors keep track of visitors and be able to compile and analyze other demographics as well? Business technology almost makes redundant some questions on the visitors' card. If visitors write down only their names and phone numbers, that's all we need. By using the Internet, we can find out where they live and even download directions to their homes. We can also use technology to do our church bulletin by e-mail. If we don't keep up with technology, the immigrants come, look around, and say, "I don't get it." Or they act as if they've stepped into an outdated church environment, and they treat us accordingly.

"The church is irrelevant" is something we've heard often in recent years. To make a positive impact on that kind of thinking, we have to be better prepared to minister in a culture where at least 10 percent of the population will abandon the physical church building for an exclusively digital faith experience. George Barna has warned, "Churches that don't make technology part of their arsenal of tools will die after the last of their antitechno members dies 20 years from now. It will be a needlessly painful death for those ministries."

As futuring leaders we know the first five things we need:

1. We prepare for change.

2. We realize we can't plan the future because the unexpected continues to happen.

3. We remain abreast of sensitive issues.

4. We become modern communicators.

5. We're not afraid of technology. In fact, we learn and use it to spread the good news of Jesus Christ.

NINE

HEALTHY LIFESTYLES

THE SIXTH TRAIT OF FUTURING leadership is what I call healthy lifestyles. In this chapter, I emphasize balance, behavior, and biotechnology.

BALANCE

I use the term balance to refer to such things as rest, proper diet, exercise, leisure, and companionship. We may never be perfectly balanced, but I believe working toward equilibrium brings us as close to being balanced people as we'll come in this age.

Because of our frazzled lifestyles today, everyone seeks balance. We're all being pulled in several directions at once. Forces outside of us jerk us around. We have more demands pulling at us today than we had yesterday, and we tend to respond to the "tyranny of the urgent," that is to the immediate cry even if it's not as important as something else. How can we alleviate stress? How can we change our behavior to handle daily crises?

We can always change our behavioral patterns. Part of balance is to remind ourselves that our bodies belong to God and that we are holy temples. We're responsible for our lifestyles, and we can do a great deal toward controlling our stress levels. We also need to remind ourselves that when we live continually stressful lives, our health and our attitude are affected as well as our effectiveness for God.

BEHAVIOR

How do I modify my behavior to meet the changing needs in my life? Above I gave the example of reaching the airport early as one stress in life that I can control. But what about my behavior when I'm with my family or at work? I behave differently with different people. At noon, for instance, I may interact with a close friend. I can laugh, plan, disagree, cry, or share and can become vulnerable in many ways. When I respond to a staff member, however, my behavior will be different. Nothing changes in respect or courtesy, but the dynamics do. When I'm talking to staff people, I am the boss. An acceptable code of behavior is in place in most situations. If I have to speak to my board, the dynamics change once again.

BIOTECHNOLOGY

Pastoral care is changing. One way to show this is to think about a brain-damaged child. In the past, parents prayed and asked for healing prayer in church, went to faith healers, or simply allowed nature to take its course. Many of them shielded their offspring from stares and ridicule by excluding them from many forms of socialization.

Today those parents take their children to a doctor who refers them to specialists. Current technology now provides life-support systems and a wide range of medication. How do we relate to such children in our churches? People today are living longer. Technology has provided a way for many people to live beyond their normal life spans. Fifty years ago, great numbers of people died in infancy. This means that we have more older people alive than at any other time in our nation's history. That alone changes the face of pastoral care.

How do we care for older parishioners? I don't mean just sending them a tape of the service along with a copy of the Sunday bulletin. Today many are in transitional homes, skilled-nursing facilities, or assisted-living environments, so how do we provide substantial pastoral care?

As futuring leaders increase their ability to grow and lead, they stress healthy lifestyles and teach others how to find balance. And as they help others cope in their struggle for balance, they become increasingly aware of their own need to make learning a lifelong practice.

TEN

LIFELONG LEARNING

THE SEVENTH TRAIT OF FUTURING leaders is that they are lifelong learners. Three significant factors about life today show a drastic shift in attitude over the generations.

1. Knowledge is power.

2. Information is currency.

3. Innovation is success.

Twenty years ago we encouraged (even pushed) our young people to get a college degree. The idea was that graduation completed formal education, and for many that is exactly the way it was. "I haven't read a book since I graduated from college," we used to hear people say with pride.

Today the degree seems less important, but learning doesn't stop. Our technological world is built on the idea of lifelong education. We can't stop learning. For instance, if my daughter earns a Master of Science in computer information systems from the most prestigious institution on this planet, within six months her education will be obsolete unless she is committed to lifelong learning.

A decade ago, some large companies could afford the luxury of paying for their employees to go to workshops, seminars, and classes to pick up continuing education units. That's no longer a luxury. If workers want to continue to do well in their jobs, they have to keep growing and learning even if they have to pay for the classes themselves.

Church leaders also need to be committed to more reading and to lifelong learning with a broader base. In the past, they read a few theological magazines— and nearly always the kind that agreed with their theological position. That's too narrow for today. Now they need to know what's going on in the world and relate to it.

Futuring leaders not only have to be aware of current Christian literature, but they also need to read or at least be conversant with non-Christian literature. There was a time when godly Christians didn't read fiction, and if they did, it was only wholesome evangelistic stories. That has changed. The proliferation and range of novels have shattered many naïve people when they have realized the broadness of the audience. Today smart leaders know what's coming off the presses in fiction and nonfiction. Because they keep up, they can answer questions about reincarnation or communicating with the dead.

Every major secular publishing house now has what they call a spiritual or Christian imprint—and well-known evangelical writers write many of the books they publish. Why this interest? It's because we're in an age of spirituality, and books on spiritual topics sell. The category spirituality, however, includes everything from yoga to Taoism to Wiccan literature to Buddhism to every aspect of Christianity.

Increasingly, niche-oriented journals are coming out. They have a faster turnaround rate and can pump out information far more quickly than book publishers.

If we're lifelong learners, not only will we be able to catch our mistakes and missteps, but we'll also be able to know what to do about correcting them. In a family, for example, lifelong learners recognize the difference between punishing and disciplining their children. Punishment is punitive; discipline is corrective and prepares them to do better next time. Punishment focuses only on behavior now, and discipline instructs for the future.

I'm thankful that God provides the best lifelong learning. In our schools and colleges, we are taught a lesson and then are tested on our own. God's way of doing things is to give us the test, stay at our side while we go through the ordeal, and gently embrace us, asking, "What have you learned from this experience?" Thus, with God our learning grows out of our testing.

Let's see how this concept works in the church by looking at styles of leadership. In the past, we accepted (and sometimes even desired) autocratic leaders. Today that style just isn't working. Some leaders keep trying, but it doesn't work for them to stand up and make pronouncements for everyone. Because they keep trying and keep failing, they are punished by lack of results. Increasingly, their critics speak out against them. The leaders themselves still haven't learned anything and one of their defenses is to resort to blame, which supposedly takes the focus off themselves and shines the spotlight on others. They say things like,

"People aren't as spiritual today as they used to be." "Church members today don't want to hear what God says."

"The Bible warns us of itching ears, and there are a lot of them in the church today."

"They're not just rejecting me, they're rejecting the Word of God."

As long as leaders blame others for their failures, see themselves as the final voice on all issues, and insist on being the leader, nothing much is going to change. However, if they listen to others, accept guidance and rebuke, and seriously study the needs of others, they will start to acknowledge that their methods just aren't effective. If they can be that open with themselves, they'll also acknowledge that failure is not because of people's hardness of heart, but because people today don't respond to a demanding style of leadership.

"How can I reframe, refocus, reinvent, or reenergize my message?" is the question futuring church leaders are asking. They no longer assume that people are indifferent, uncaring, and stiff-necked. Instead, they figure out what people don't respond to and recognize that it was often their style of leadership. As they continue to learn, they ask, "What approach can I take that people will understand and accept as supportive? How can I do ministry differently?" They may even say to themselves, "Maybe I need a champion—someone who can support my cause."

Changing leadership styles is a real test for many leaders because they have always been at the center of all activity and they're uncomfortable if they're not in charge. One thing they'll learn is that it doesn't matter who gets credit for initiating ideas or even carrying them out. The effective results are what count.

Not all leadership styles can accommodate that openness, but it's something I've learned to do. I think it's because, when I pastored, I learned that instead of thinking of leadership as power, I functioned better if I considered leadership as influence. The best leaders are those who motivate, suggest, and encourage but who don't demand, tell, or insist.

KNOWLEDGE IS POWER

At different times in history, people have perceived power differently. For example, a century ago in the Old West, a rancher showed power by counting heads of cattle. A decade ago, churches showed their influence and prestige by the number of buses in their parking lot. Our perceptions are changing. Although we've long been aware of the importance of knowledge, it is only within recent years that we have seen that knowledge (or information as it is sometimes called) is power.

We've always known that knowledge is power, of course, but it's truer than ever today. One thing leaders especially need to know, however, is that they don't have to know everything. When I was growing up, we lived by the unwritten law of the church that the pastor knew everything, the elders and deacons knew almost as much, and the people knew little. Not only did everyone assume that church leaders had to know everything; they also had to have the answers to every question, and they had to have at least two Bible verses to prove their point.

One of the most freeing experiences for any pastor is to say to the congregation, "I don't know." This becomes even more powerful when the same pastor says to elders and deacons, "Do you know what we should do? What's your opinion?" (This is just as true for leadership on every level. It's such a relief to students in Sunday school, for instance, when the teacher says, "I have no idea.")

To acknowledge ignorance not only frees pastors and other leaders from heavy burdens they can't carry, but it also frees them up to be human beings. In the process, people actually get to know them as fallible, and they can identify more readily with them as individuals. This confession invites others to share in the process of dealing with problematic situations.

We're living with what I call relational challenges. When we share information or allow others to share their information with us, we build bridges. We become vulnerable, but that's not the real issue. We enhance our authenticity and our credibility as we allow others to open up to us and we open up to them.

By contrast, imagine what it would be like in church if

- the organist or pianist discovered beautiful chords but didn't want to give the music away lest others play as well as he or she does.

- the youth pastor knew of a strategic influencer who had helped greatly to advance a certain program, but held that information so that no one else would know and take advantage of the same source.

INFORMATION IS CURRENCY

In our world, information is the best currency. We barter information, and our information increases by sharing it. As soon as I give it away, I've increased it by giving it to someone else, who can then give it away and increase it even more. I'm not worried about who else is going to take that material and keep it.

It saddens me that pastors, elders, deacons, and teachers know things they don't pass on to their people. They would be more effective if they would share more. One principle I apply to sharing information involves asking, "Who else needs to know this?" As soon as I begin to read a new piece of information that comes across my desk, I ask, "Who else can benefit from this?"

One of my roles as a Bible college president is to bring in funds for programs not covered by tuition. Most people would reason that we should keep our sources as secret as possible so that no one else would tap the same wallet or purse and thereby would cut off any future help for us. I don't believe that! In fact, once I share openly, the results amaze me. When I introduce my funders to somebody else who needs funding, we all become winners. This may not make sense to many people, but it works, and I've been advocating it for a long time. When someone comes to me needing money for a project I believe in, I point that person to someone who can help. I've shared such information dozens of times, and I've never lost anything. Every time I've done this, our funding has actually increased from the same source.

I've given away information and built a bridge, and everyone profited. Jesus laid down the principle: "If you give, you will receive. Your gift will return to you in full measure. . . . Whatever measure you use in giving—large or small—it will be used to measure what is given back to you" (Luke 6:38–39 NLT). Since Jesus set the example and gave the instructions I can give away sources and resources.

As a leader, I have chosen to work through people, so not only am I asking, "Who else can benefit from what I know?" but I'm also asking, "Who can help me?" Once I answer those questions, I am in the process of building a strategic team.

INNOVATION IS SUCCESS

Innovation answers the question, "What can we do that nobody else is doing?" That is a very difficult and courageous question to ask. Those grappling with the issues of the futuring church must look carefully at their demographics and use that information to determine what kind of services or ministries they need to offer and the kind of people they need to staff them.

Furthermore, they must determine what skills people need for new services or ministries. For example, if I had been a youth leader five years ago and my competency hadn't increased, I wouldn't be able to relate effectively to today's youth. Yet I find too many still focusing on the traditional methods of the past. They promote youth camp, VBS, and youth rallies— and none of those things are wrong or bad; they're just a bit outdated. Innovative programs are more family oriented, and activities are scheduled only for evening hours.

We must offer more than just a Sunday morning service that includes praise and worship, an offering, and a sermon. Instead, we need to offer innovative ministries that meet the needs of the people. Here's something else. Small groups have changed. It used to be that we set up small groups/cell groups/ home groups by zip codes. Now we establish groups by interests. For example, one group of teens may want to play basketball, another may want to go fishing, another golfing, and yet another walking around the mall. I visited a church that offered five-week courses on gourmet cooking, landscaping, small business start-up, and art instruction. The classes were packed, and many who attended were not church members.

I like to think of these kinds of programs as innovation in the midst of tradition. Churches that innovate move along with speed. They don't bog down new ideas by referring them to feasibility committees. They don't get overwhelmed and discouraged because a few Christians ask every time they present a new idea, "What are we going to get out of this?"

But, as Christians, we are called to serve others. Therefore, as leaders, we have to help people like this deacon change their thinking. Instead of ignoring their questions, because they ask out of their sense of need and their understanding of the gospel, we should try what I call oblique thinking. Oblique thinking would say to those who ask such questions, "You know, there may be some truth in that." Then we need to follow up with our own question: "How do we bridge the gap? How do we manifest the love of Jesus Christ and serve others?"

I've suggested to several congregational leaders that they approach the situation differently. That gets away from asking, "What do we get out of this?" They begin by sending money to support a homeless shelter. Get people in the church to think about such places and pray for the ministry to the homeless. After a period of time, designate a day once a month when members of the congregation visit the shelter to serve people food, talk with them, and wash dishes.

When we engage in these projects, we may never receive even one new member. It's not likely that the homeless people will come and worship with us. But even when we don't see measurable results, we have followed the example of Jesus, reached out with compassion, and shown kindness and caring.

ELEVEN

CREATIVE LEADERSHIP

T HE EIGHTH TRAIT OF FUTURING LEADERS is creative leadership. The word creativity may scare some. It means thinking outside the box and coloring outside the lines. It means daring to look around and envision what lies ahead. And it means questioning the old ways and asking, "Is there a newer, more efficient method?" Most futuring leaders do this instinctively, but all of us can also learn to think creatively.

Thinking creatively is one of futuring leaders' primary responsibilities. For things to happen, they have to dream and see the impossible as within their grasp. But too often the people who most need to think creatively lock themselves into one style of thinking. Instead, they need to incorporate three kinds of thinking—strategic, genius, and oblique.

STRATEGIC THINKING

Strategic thinking is another name for logical or analytic thinking. We are at point A, and we want to reach point B and then move to C and on to D. This kind of visioning asks basic questions that can't be avoided:

- Who is going to do it? When will it get done?
- How much is it going to cost?
- Who is going to be accountable for this project?
- What are the marks of success and failure?
- How do we evaluate the success or failure of the venture?
- How do we know that we want to move from B to C? Do we stay at B? Should we skip C and go to D?

GENIUS THINKING

Genius thinking goes beyond strategic thinking. It begins by recognizing the available resources but it also recognizes that the resources are limited.

Strategic thinking says, "This is what we have to work with, and this is what we are going to do. This is the amount of money we need, the number of people involved, and the building we require." The plan is laid out logically. Genius thinking starts at this point and seeks possibilities that others haven't considered. I like to think of it this way: The difference between a leader and a manager is that managers work with or "manage" resources that are given to them by leaders.

Leaders say, "We need more space and more workers. Now let's see what we can do to get more." They search for creative ways to resource themselves. This isn't to say that we don't need managers—we do—but we need leaders first and managers to come in behind and support them. No one should say that a leader is more important than a manager. If someone were to ask me which is more important, I'd have to respond with my own question: "What wing of the airplane is more important to keep it flying? The left or the right?"

For us in the futuring church, growth management is a tremendous challenge. Genius thinking sees possibilities and says, "We can make that happen." Too often native thinking says, "Let's send it to a committee for recommendations."

Genius thinking also rephrases concepts. For example, I don't use the word problem. I prefer the word challenge. By changing our use of just one word, we present a different picture in people's minds. Problems easily lead to dead ends or at least to a lot of struggling. Challenges give us opportunities to overcome hindrances.

Another sentence, again not original, that my staff uses often is "The difficult we do at once, the impossible takes a little longer." This challenges them not to throw up their hands and roll their eyes but to say, "We don't know what to do—yet."

OBLIQUE THINKING

Oblique thinking looks for options that are neither white nor black. Most of the time, people think in terms of either/or when they could be thinking both/and.

There was a time when churches decided to relocate that one of the first things leaders said was "We need to sell this present building before we can build another." Oblique thinking says, "This is a transitional community, and we need to relocate. That's obvious. For us to relocate, do we have to sell this present building?" The answer is "No, we don't have to sell." Oblique thinking asks, "Why can't we use the present facilities as a mission base? Why can't we become part of another church that is already in this area? Why can't we resource them?"

Another innovation that is a result of oblique thinking is that we see shared facilities all over the country. One building may house congregations that hold services in English, Korean, and Spanish. Why would we want to construct a building and invest at least a million dollars for cathedral ceilings and ornate glass windows for only two and a half hours a week? Is that good stewardship? Instead, oblique thinking asks, "What else can this money be used for?"

We must always keep asking ourselves, "What else can we do?" When we think in that way, we are more aware of the needs of others. We consider what we can do to help people outside the church so that together we can break down the walls that divide us.

Someone once said, "The greatest pleasure in life is doing what people think can't be done." I do know that creativity can make things happen that no one thought about before.

TWELVE

TIMING

THE NINTH TRAIT OF FUTURING LEADERSHIP is timing. The past is prologue, the present is action now, and the future shows the results of our present decisions. All of this is par for the course. Prologue. The past provides background and reminds us of where we've been. No matter how much we remember, we cannot change or improve the past.

Action takes place in the present, but we direct those decisions toward the future. Results refer totally to the future, because we can't foresee the outcome when we make our decisions. The space between the past and the future closes almost instantly. By that I mean that we're always living and working in the future. We're never in the past. Most of us are barely in the present. As soon as we blink, we're into the future that we thought about only minutes ago.

As we think about timing, it helps if we make this a motto of our thinking: The past is prologue. That is, when we look backward, we gain insight into the background, the reasons for particular actions, and the needs that brought about such decisions.

The past is over. We can do nothing to improve the past. Obviously, our actions must take place in the present. But that's not enough, because our actions must be grounded in the future. That is, actions taken right now can't simply be for the matter of expediency or to get rid of a pressing challenge. Whatever decisions and choices we make will have implications for and results in the future, and we need to be aware of what they will be.

That is especially significant when we talk about long-range planning. I smile as I think about the term long-range planning. During my college days and into my pastoral years, we constantly heard about looking far ahead and making plans for the next decade. We thought in large blocks of at least five years and often projected that to ten or fifteen or even twenty. That's outmoded and impossible today because of the rapidity of change in our world. Today the outer limits on long-range planning are three years—and even that may be too far ahead and need corrections.

Fast-moving, rapidly growing churches do what they call "annual planning"—but they do the planning at quarterly meetings. Is it any wonder they're growing? They're staring into the immediate future. They also incorporate preparedness, an even better concept than long-range planning. Their goal is to be ready now for what happens next week or anywhere up ahead.

Being prepared for the future is more important than planning for it. If an opportunity comes to us today, we must be ready—right now—to move on it. Decisions that used to go to committees and then subcommittees and sometimes feasibility groups sometimes took three years before being finalized. Life isn't waiting that long today.

Let's suppose I'm a pastor in a growing church and our present facilities are filled to capacity. From a realtor friend, I learn about a piece of land that is on the market today. It's valuable and it's in the perfect location. "This land won't stay available," he says. "I've already had three other calls." Because he's my friend, he says, "Here's what I'll do. I'll hold this property until 3:00 this afternoon. If I don't receive a bid from you by then, don't bother to call me later." What do I do? What can I do? Do I, as a pastor, have the power to act? Is there someone I can call who has the authority to act? Must I wait to call a board meeting and then appoint a committee?

Too late! The land is already gone. If our church is in a state of preparation, we can act. If we're still doing long-range planning, we probably aren't even aware that we'll need to buy new land. That's the way our world operates today. Everything rushes down the fast track.

Let's go back to the challenge of available land. A futuring church would have foreseen the need for larger facilities at least a year in advance of the land's availability. They would already have been watching and waiting for the right piece of real estate to go on the market. And because they were prepared, they would have empowered someone to act immediately.

PLANNING AHEAD

What we see now has value. It has the same value as my rear-view and side-view mirrors, which tell me where I've been and if something is coming up behind me. But we can't drive with our eyes focused on what we've already passed. We keep thinking we can look backward and see how it was done once and then adapt it for the future. That just doesn't work.

Let's say I live in an area that is rapidly transitioning from a single-home community into an apartment community. That's the future, so everything I do now has to interface with that reality. If I know that my community is getting younger because families with small children are moving in, I also realize that our church has an opportunity to gain more young families. To make that happen, our church will need a playground for those children as well as a well-equipped nursery and staff. We also will need to ask ourselves, "What else can we offer that will attract these new families?"

As far as I'm concerned, the most vital places in and around the church—beginning with their order of importance—are:

- First, the nursery.
- Second, the ladies' room.
- Third, the foyer.
- Fourth, the parking lot.
- Fifth, the sanctuary.

This order may surprise some. One person challenged me on the foyer as third. It is, however, the place where members have fellowship and build relationships. It's where small talk opens the way for more significant talk later. If we have a narrow, small, dark, or dingy foyer, it's functional—like a cattle chute. But people don't want to talk in a crowded hallway where they are constantly being bumped. If we provide a larger, well-lit space as a foyer, people are more likely to congregate and chat with each other.

Since we're looking at the future to see the kind of people who will attend our church, suppose we consider the needs of the growing senior population. How will our facilities fit their needs? Modern church planning requires serious architectural study, and a key consideration is space for expansion. Thus, most new church development is being done in three phases. First, they construct the building for worship; then they expand the auditorium; and finally, they erect a balcony—something that went out of fashion two generations ago and is now making a comeback. Many new church buildings are being constructed with high ceilings so that a balcony can be added if necessary.

PRACTICAL PLANNING

Suppose I walked into a room with ten pastors present and asked, "What will your church look like ten years from now?"

I don't think many of them would know. I don't know either, but I could help them, because I know where they do their best thinking. It starts with what happened in the past. I've done this many times, and the results are about the same on each occasion.

I ask them to take out two sheets of paper and I say, "On the first page, I want you to list ten major changes that have taken place within the past decade of your ministry." I wait and they write. Within a few minutes, they've completed that list, because it's easy to write. Then I say, "Using that material to help you do your thinking, on the second page, write a list of changes you foresee within the next five years."

They stare at me. Sometimes they leave the page blank. They may scribble a few words, but few of them know how to answer the question. My point is this: Too many church leaders spend most of their time fixing the past and managing the present, so they can't make time to prepare for the future.

Remember, the past is prologue, the present is action, and the future is results. This forms an acrostic:

Prologue—the past is done. And no one can improve it.

Action takes place in the present. But it points toward the future.

Results are in the future and reveal what will be achieved.

All of this is par for the course.

We have discussed nine significant characteristics that futuring leaders need to develop. In chapter 13, we will discover one more powerful element they need to incorporate. They need to look ahead, peek over the horizon, and be ready for what lies ahead.

THIRTEEN
FUTURE GAZING

THE TENTH TRAIT OF FUTURING leadership is future gazing. Futuring church leaders forecast trends, envision scenarios, and help to create the desired future. To reach that desired future, we have to shift our thinking. We can no longer stumble along and trust that somehow the Spirit of God will intervene and lead us into the Promised Land of excitement and spiritual growth.

The Bible is quite clear that God gives the growth, but it also tells us that God uses people to prepare the fields and plant the seed. When we have done what we can, then God does indeed give the increase and also completes the tasks that we, as humans, can't do. Paul says it this way: "I planted the seed, Apollos watered it, but God made it grow" (1 Cor. 3:6).

Well-known writer Henry Blackaby has encouraged us to ask the all-important question, "Where are you going, God?" Then we go where God is going instead of inviting him to go along with our plans.

Successful futuring churches don't just happen, even though God sometimes blesses in spite of our ignorance or lack of planning. Doesn't it make sense to follow God's way—to seek God's guidance each step of the way?

As I've been stressing all through this book, if we want to give ourselves the highest possibilities not just for survival but also for growth, we need leaders who prepare for the future.

That makes staffing a primary issue. We used to work on a simple system. We had a solo pastor. Then as the church grew, we hired an assistant to take over the youth work; or in some churches, the second staff person did educational work. If the congregation continued to grow, we hired another person to do specialized ministry. We had paid choir directors, organists, and pianists. That's what we needed in 1930, and we still needed them in 1980. What do we need now?

Instead of opting for a young minister or assistant pastor, futuring churches hire a person they call by various terms, such as "spiritual development director," to be responsible for developing spirituality within the congregation. And some churches no longer hire choir directors. That's too narrow a focus. Instead, they seek someone who can incorporate music, dance, and drama in worship services.

Futuring leaders have recognized that it's not enough to minister to the youth; they need to find ways to impact the parents and other family members. Therefore, they hire those who can establish and teach family foundations by working with entire families.

Another characteristic of growing churches is that they now have executive or administration pastors, although the term may not always be used. These pastors deal only with the administrative responsibilities of the congregation. A church doesn't call such pastors to preach or teach but to do administrative work, because that's their gift. They take care of the business of the church, such as staffing, budgeting, and other routine matters.

At a church leadership conference, Leonard Sweet said that we no longer live in the land of the status quo; we live in the land of status flux. He called it a seascape, because, unlike the landscape where our feet rest on solid ground and we can predict future events, we live in what he calls an "aquaculture" where everything is in constant change.

I've spelled out ten characteristics of futuring leaders. In the next chapter, I look at the trends we need to face that remind us, "This ain't your daddy's church." Although our foundation is secure in Jesus Christ, the struggles we face are new. To be aware of these trends is to begin seeking ways of coping with them.

FOURTEEN
FORTY-FOUR TRENDS*

CHURCH LEADERS HAVE SPOTTED SOME trends in American churches that we believe will continue. Some are further along than others, but within five years these changes probably will have occurred. Some are happening in mainline denominations, and most are emerging among independent congregations. Regardless, they are happening—now.

I'm listing these trends because congregations need to take action on them. We can't act on or react to anything we don't know about. As you read this chapter, my hope is that your thinking will become more flexible and you will consider ways to respond to these challenges. To get this picture more clearly, let's try to imagine ourselves going to sleep in 1963 and waking up in 2003.

We walk up to a church deacon and ask, "What has changed?"

---

* I do not advocate, endorse, or encourage the trends discussed in this chapter. They will, however, serve as catalysts for futuring.

"Everything has changed," he answers. "Yes, but specifically, what has changed?"

He tells us about advances in technology and transportation, changes in the family structure, how houses are now being built and where they're located. He talks about cell phones, the commute structure, and the entertainment industry. The list becomes almost endless.

Here's the tragedy in this scenario: Most of our churches went to sleep decades ago. Even though they appear to be awake, they're oblivious to changes that have taken place in the culture that affect the church. I can say that without hesitation because I've visited hundreds of congregations since the beginning of the new millennium that show no significant changes in their worship experiences over the past forty years.

The good news is that churches are waking up—and part of the reason for that awakening is that we're being forced to shake ourselves and go through serious self-examination. The tendency, of course, is to want to return to the way things were before. If we open our eyes wide, like Rip Van Winkle did after he had slept for twenty years, and return to our village, we're faced with a shocking reality: Nothing has remained the same. Like Van Winkle, we're tempted to throw our energy into making time go backward, but it's impossible.

That's the tension we face today. We long for the simpler ways and the clear-cut choices between right and wrong. "In the good old days," we had few questions about morals and the role of authority figures. Now we have to shift our thinking. Tensions increase as we examine the wide gap between what things used to be, what they have become, and what the gap will be in another decade.

It's a shame that we haven't been sensitive to the prompting of the Holy Spirit so that we could become the change leaders in the world. In fact, it's the reverse. Serious transformations in society are forcing the awakening church to reexamine itself. And we tend to scream, groan, and grumble the whole time.

The forty-four trends are listed in random order because I'm not sure of their importance. In various parts of the country, believers will see one issue as having higher priority than other areas—that's another drastic shift from forty-plus years ago.

1. Denominations are not an issue. There was a time when, if Baptists moved to Seattle from Chicago and were in search of a new church, they considered only Baptist churches. That is no longer true. The same held true for Presbyterians, Methodists, and independents. This trend of putting less importance on denominations has been going on for at least twenty-five years, but it is becoming important enough that denominational leaders are studying it seriously.

Many people prefer a style of worship, and the denominational tag means little. If we drive by newer church structures, we find an interesting phenomenon. Fifty years ago the denomination name stood out in large letters. Today some churches are putting their denominational affiliation on their signs in small letters or leaving it off all together. Immigrants may visit a church and not even realize they're in a Missouri Synod Lutheran or Pentecostal Holiness church.

When natives move, they still seek "our church." Immigrants, however, don't look for the closest Methodist church, although they're not averse to joining one. They're more caught up in pragmatic issues:

- How convenient is it to get there?
- How many miles is it from our house?
- What services do they offer?
- Do they have family programs and youth activities?

Perhaps unconsciously immigrants seek a particular leadership style. They may not be able to define it, but they recognize it when they find it. They seek interaction that will be available to them at their choosing. They may choose not to be heavily involved, and they don't want to attend a congregation where they're made to feel guilty for not subscribing to all the tenets of the church. They want to hold many options.

The basic beliefs, such as the statement of faith, may still be important, but the form of worship, style of ministry, and the warmth (or lack of it) among members take preeminence over theological issues.

Virtually unheard of a few years ago, today thousands of Christians will go to another denomination's church that doesn't subscribe to all the tenets they have been used to. Check out any growing congregation and ask how many are natives to that denomination. It's amazing how few are. It's equally amazing how many have come from a variety of other backgrounds.

Immigrants know that life involves trade-offs. No one church can offer them everything they want. They know they'll never have all they are looking for. So if the church they visit has a good program for their children, they are willing to make trade-offs—and the theological differences seem less important than the care of their children.

2. The term home church has no relevance. Natives thought of exclusive and long-term membership in one congregation. Immigrants are shoppers for the faith, and they seek short-term relationships with several congregations.

There was a time when we'd meet other Christians and one of the first questions we would ask was, "What's your home church?" We could use that to label them— not in a negative sense. When we heard the answer, we knew how to respond and how to direct the conversation from there. It was a useful get-acquainted device. Today that question is increasingly unlikely to provide answers. Because immigrants have become shoppers for the faith, they don't feel tied down with longterm relationships with a single congregation. Natives are aghast, but immigrants have not bought into the idea of church loyalty. In fact, many immigrants join with a congregation assuming they will experience a short-term relationship.

Typically, natives stress duty. They feel an obligation to stay in one church. They teach a Sunday school class year after year. Or they volunteer to help in the nursery, and fifteen years later, they're still there. Natives were raised in a society where duty and obligation were key culture words.

Today, duty is dead and obligation is unemployed. How does the futuring church get around this trend? The old method was for those in the pulpit to induce guilt. When natives considered leaving, leaders preached and taught to make them struggle with questions such as, "What will people think?" and "Will we be failing God if we stop ushering every Sunday?" Because of the short-term mind-set, guilt doesn't work anymore. Immigrants have multiple needs, and our culture encourages them to be service driven, getting what they can from different places. They might go to one church on Wednesday nights because that church has an excellent program for their teens. On Sunday morning they attend another church as a family because they like the outstanding choir or the powerful preaching. They also might enroll in small groups and be with people they don't attend church with.

Years ago many churches developed the idea of cell groups or neighborhood gatherings to keep their members focused on the church. That's not the way it works today. Immigrants may become regular members of a cell group only because it meets a specific need they have.

What about Christian leaders whose responsibilities don't allow them to worship at their church regularly? Can they have a purpose and function in that church? In my own case, I'm certain to be at my home church on Easter, Mother's Day, and Christmas but not on many other Sundays.

3. Cell churches (we used to call them home groups or neighborhood Bible studies) are changing. Because people in our society have become so disconnected from one another, there is an even greater inner need to be connected. That disconnection has highlighted the need for community. Immigrants want to be attached to small groups, so growing larger churches break their members down into smaller groups. The purpose of small groups isn't to grow a church, but to grow the person.

Previously, churches divided home groups by zip codes and neighborhoods because they focused on the convenience of driving or walking within the neighborhood. Geographic convenience no longer holds the appeal. Instead, the trend is to emphasize age and areas of interest, such as Bible study, music, golfing, fishing, shopping, and parenting.

The old cell groups used to be Bible-study based. The trend is now toward relationships. Is the Bible involved? Yes. Do they have Bible studies? Yes, they do—but they're different. If immigrants get together for two hours twice a month, they may spend fifteen or twenty minutes in structured Bible study. The rest of the time is directional or applicational, and especially they seek guidance on ethical issues.

"What does the Bible say about nuclear war?"

"Our daughter wants her boyfriend to live with her in our house. What do I do?"

"How are we supposed to relate to our Muslim neighbors?" These are real-life struggles and challenges.

Today's church members want to talk about their families, challenges they face in the workplace, events in their lives, and transitions they're involved in.

"Is there somebody else out there who's going through what I'm going through? If so, can we talk about it?" may be the approach.

Thus, the essence of the cell group has changed from church based and Bible study based, to relationship based and affinity group based.

4. People are involved in the church without attending each Sunday. Growing churches will have people who are serious about their level of spirituality but without a Sunday-go-to-meeting attitude. Their concern is "How do I live my faith during the week? How do I apply what I'm learning?"

The relationship between serving God and attending church every Sunday doesn't mean the same to immigrants as it does for natives. Immigrants are strong about living out their spirituality, but they don't think they have to be in church every week to do that.

Immigrants see their spiritual lives like this: One day they're fully involved at Grace Assembly. They may not be sitting in church the next week, but it doesn't mean they're not serving the Lord. It simply means that the relationship between serving God and attending church every Sunday doesn't hold the same meaning for immigrants that it does for natives.

For us natives, something was wrong if we didn't attend church at least three out of four Sundays each month. People just didn't consider us spiritual or committed to Christ.

5. High spirituality and low organized religion mark futuring church congregations. Natives were taught to live their spirituality through the opportunities for service within their own congregation. Modern spirituality is lived out Monday through Sunday and much of that outside the context of organized religion or through parachurch, faith-based community outreach.

If immigrants want to disinfect mattresses at a homeless shelter, they'll do it even if it's not on their church's to-do list. They might choose to become involved in programs sponsored by their local church, but they're not limited to them.

In the past, organized religion would say, "Come to church. Be involved in our programs. This is what we offer and what's going on." Spirituality was lived out through the worship experience or opportunities for service.

Spirituality is now being lived out at a different level. Immigrants consider it a higher level, because they live their faith Monday through Sunday and do most of it outside the context of organized religion or beyond the walls of a single church. Natives, however, have limited themselves to saying, "Our church does this. These are the programs we're involved in."

6. Worship service days and times vary. The two fastest growing types of churches in America are those that have church services that begin no later than 8:30 Sunday morning (some as early as 7:30) and those that offer worship on Friday or Saturday evening.

In fact, Friday or Saturday evening services attract more of the unreached. Christians can invite others much more easily. "Let's go to church tonight. It'll start at 6:30, and we'll be out by 8:00. Why don't our families get together for dinner after that?" This fits the immigrant lifestyle, because they don't want to tie up their entire weekend for a church service. This way they can go in, worship, and have the rest of the weekend free.

7. Worship structures are changing. In the past, most churches operated about the same way, with a call to worship, three hymns, the offering, Bible reading, and a sermon. The challenge—and demand—is for nontraditional formats. Ministers over forty were trained in biblical competence and theological scholarship, but not in storytelling and listening—the demands of immigrants.

We're learning that telling and retelling stories—including biblical stories—can be very powerful.

Short attention spans are evident in our church pews, so the service has to be done in what I call snippets. That is, worship elements need to be continually changing. Music, drama, and multimedia presentations are interspersed with preaching. Television has conditioned us to expect to receive information in sound bites. That means the church service has to keep moving with no dead moments.

For instance, wise medical people know that. If we visit a savvy doctor, we'll sit in the outside waiting room for a maximum of ten minutes before a receptionist calls our name and ushers us into the inside waiting room. We'll have perhaps another five-minute wait before a nurse comes in and talks to us or takes our blood pressure—some small thing—and then she leaves. This is the pattern. We may have to wait a total of forty-five minutes to an hour, but we have enough happening every few minutes that it doesn't seem as if it's that long.

It also seems as if several people are involved in our case and they keep us moving.

8. Worship styles are changing. Worship style will define the congregation. Singing about God has shifted to singing to God. Many new choruses and praise hymns may not be theologically correct, but they have the style and tempo people want to sing. Futuring churches are trying to incorporate the span of music from pipe organ to rap—all in one service.

The worship team/choir/music department provides a great challenge for any pastor. I've heard some people joke that when the first choir director, Lucifer, fell, he fell right into the choir loft. And there hasn't been any peace since then.

The biggest challenge is for families. Teenagers like one kind of music and their parents like something else, but parents tend to defer to the children because they're willing to do a trade-off. As a parent, I'd rather go to church with my children and have them enjoy it than expect them to put up with music they hate. Increasingly, churches will adapt in a number of different ways. It's now common to have different types of services. Friday night could be a contemporary casual format. Early Sunday morning could be traditional and liturgical.

I preached one Sunday at Evangel Church in Chicago. Their first service, which they called the "Get Up Service," was fairly traditional. They called the second one the "Get Down Service." In that service, one choir number lasted a half hour (I timed it), but it had a lot of variation and included congregational participation.

This says that futuring leaders are offering different experiences, and people are attending the services in which the worship style and format fit most of their preferences.

9. Evangelism takes place in both seeker-sensitive as well as more blatant forms. Bill Hybels popularized seeker-sensitive evangelism at Willow Creek, but it's not the only format. Direct, in-your-face evangelism is still being used by growing churches as well.

We don't need to take sides on how to do evangelism. Various styles work depending on the cultural context. I do know this: Immigrants don't want us to play around. "Tell us what you need or what you want to do. Then I'll tell you whether I'm going to respond." They seem to have no problem saying, "No, I don't think I want to do that right now."

10. Revival comes in different forms. Revival itself is being redefined. It used to be the term for a church holding protracted or evangelistic services. Revival now simply means that people who are a part of the community of believers are empowered to live out the life of Christ in their daily living.

Revivals don't always take place inside the church building; they can happen where people live, work, and play as well. They ask, "How can I live out my faith each day?" Immigrants also understand that corporate revival can only happen if individual revival is in place.

When a native prays, "Send us a revival, Lord; send us a revival," he or she is referring to the Lord working in church services. An important evangelist is going to come in and preach, and "People are going to get saved, the church is going to grow and be alive, and we're going to have a great time." After the evangelist leaves, the revival is over. For the immigrant, revival means, "So now I can learn how to live the faith I have. I'll learn how to transmit my faith to my neighbor."

11. The church develops rather than trains. Training is task oriented—a short-term focus on a job that needs to be done. Development focuses more on the person rather than the task, is long term, and is process driven rather than event driven.

Churches that used to do training assumed that if they taught someone how to be an usher, that's all that person did. Those people were good, well-trained ushers. Today these churches develop person-centered abilities and teach people conflict resolution and trouble-shooting skills. In their systemic thinking, they develop them as individuals who have multiple skills, and those same skills can be used in many different places instead of just one defined area.

12. Education for the church is moving from teaching to learning. Teaching focuses on the teacher, but learning focuses on the students. When a church looks at its Christian education department, it needs to ask, "What are people learning?" That is, they begin from the end, and their goals drive them.

With approval of the voucher system, home schools will increase along with Christian schools. Future-oriented churches are asking, "How do we hook up with the home school?"

They answer, "Provide a gym, a library, and a music program. Home schoolers need places for social interaction, and their parents need support groups." Future churches are figuring out how to reach out to home schoolers—even those without religious affiliation—and offer assistance with no strings attached. They hook into home school associations in their neighborhood and open church facilities to them, especially the gym. Parents can hold meetings at the church and can establish a good library. The only expense for the church is utilities. Imagine the outreach to the community because home schoolers have a place they can call theirs with no strings attached.

Christian education in futuring churches emphasizes interactive, integrated, and individualized learning. Interactive means there must be a connection between what is being taught and the real world. The stress on individualized instruction demands smaller classrooms, more one-on-one instruction, more parental involvement, and more volunteerism.

The criteria used to be that students studied their Sunday school quarterlies and learned the weekly memory verses. Now the emphasis is "What have you learned that is changing your life? In what ways are you now different because of the lessons?"

The Christian school movement is continuing to grow but in a different way. Previously only large churches had Christian schools; now smaller churches are beginning Christian schools as well. They are more objective or criteria driven, which means teachers will need to know clearly what they are trying to achieve each term or semester. They also need to show how this new knowledge integrates with real life.

No longer is it enough to teach arithmetic just as problems for students to work through. Teachers are now posing real-life issues. "If you go to Kroger with x amount of money and shop…" Or "You open a savings account at a local bank and…"

Instead of teaching only addition and subtraction, we've seen the need to teach people how to balance their checkbooks. We know two things about Americans and their checking accounts. First, most Americans accept the figures on their bank statements without verifying them. Second, many of them don't know how to reconcile their bank statements with their checkbooks. Teaching people how to balance their checkbooks is important, because, as stewardship institutes have taught us, people who regularly balance their checkbooks are better givers.

I visited one large academy for grades pre-K through six. Every classroom has three computers, and they have an Internet-active computer lab. Charles Schwab, the investing company, has partnered with the school and set up every classroom with a business that seeded the class a small amount of money, about one hundred dollars. Each class has had to devise a business plan and sell a product. Money earned is divided among the stockholders of the company—the students. If they want to spin off another company, the stockholders can decide not to take the money but to invest it. That's integrated learning in the real world.

I also see in the future smaller, more individualized classrooms with higher levels of parent involvement and more volunteerism.

13. Leadership teams replace single leaders. "None of us is as good as all of us." In the past, one person led everything, but immigrants want to be part of the leadership team.

As I've mentioned elsewhere, there was a time when the pastor stood behind the pulpit and said, "Thus saith the Lord," and most of the church members went along without question. Today's immigrants want to be part of a winning team. Therefore, they are willing to take orders from a coach and change their style of playing to win the game. They are not, however, willing to submit to autocratic control. That means that in futuring churches, dialogue comes before decision. The process is more important than the destination.

14. Decisions are made by consensus. Futuring churches hand down fewer executive decisions and try to operate by consensus instead. Leaders aren't trying to get people to announce whether they're for or against anything. Rather, they work until there is general agreement. They're trying to get everyone to see the larger picture. Once that happens, wisdom emerges for the greater good.

15. Church governments are changing. Church boards and committees are being replaced by teams, and within the teams are subgroups or task forces: Task forces have the ability to make faster short- and long-term decisions, because they have one task to do and that's the end of their responsibility. Churches that are going to reach and hold the dot.com crowd can't wait two years to make a decision. They're risk takers, and they want change now. The essence of their thinking is that if they wait one more day, they are that much farther behind.

16. The church is being forced to rethink sexuality. The three major issues are women in ministry, homosexuality, and abortion. Other issues include cohabitation outside of marriage and women choosing to have a family without having relations with a man. Churches need to define their stand on such issues, and the best time to do so is when they are not involved with one of these problems. The best time to talk about something is when there's nothing to talk about. No church is going to be exempt from all of these issues, no matter how biblical the church might view itself to be.

17. The demand for excellence increases. In preaching, the demand for excellence isn't on the knowledge of biblical languages and polished illustrations. Immigrants seek authenticity and integrity. In teaching, they demand substance and not the lightweight material we have used in recent years. The third demand is for relevance— preaching with the Bible in one hand and the newspaper in the other.

18. Church leaders are being held to stricter requirements. It's still relatively easy to join a congregation, but those who aspire to leadership will face heavier demands. The church I attend has a weekly attendance of 180 to 190 every Sunday. Even though small, we have leadership development meetings for everyone in any type of leadership. It's done in phases, and those who haven't completed phase one may not go on to phase two. No one can serve in leadership before completing phase two. Five years ago, going through such a program was voluntary; it is now required.

I've also observed that many futuring churches make covenants built around what I call the "what-ifs." Such a covenant will spell out requirements for being a leader and consequences for failing to meet those requirements. For example, if a leader fails to tithe, such and such will happen.

When immigrants are being serviced, they want to know that those who serve them are competent. They know that competency means continuous learning. Why, for example, would a church let me teach Sunday school if I had never been through all the necessary training? If I'm in computers, I have to keep going to school all the time. If I'm a dentist or a heart surgeon, I have to keep up with new technology. So in the mind of immigrants, it makes sense for leaders to be on the cutting edge.

Because many immigrants are unwilling to join (they don't want to obligate themselves), some churches are willing to use nonmembers—as long as they have been through the required training process.

19. Immigrants seek a vision and purpose-driven church. They ask church leaders, "What is your purpose? Why are you here?" They want to devote their time, energy, and resources to worthwhile projects. When immigrants consider giving to the Lord, the local church isn't usually their first thought, which runs contrary to the thinking of natives. Immigrants take their resources to where they see people of vision and purpose wisely using them.

20. Discipline in the church is expected and implemented. In the working world, there are consequences for failing to do quality work. The church also expects competence. Formerly in the church, discipline was a bad word, but that's changing. Churches generally have a set of guidelines for leaders. If they don't meet those standards of competence, they do not stay in leadership. Sunday school teachers, for example, are required to attend quarterly teacher training classes. If they don't, they are removed. The word then gets out that the church has high standards. They want their teachers to be well qualified for what they are doing. And they want parents to feel that they can entrust their children to those teachers.

21. Relevancy is in demand. Immigrants ask, "Why?" Church leaders can no longer say, "Everyone knows that. . . . " We have to explain things to immigrants, because they may question what natives took for granted. And native leaders need to understand that immigrants' questions aren't signs of disagreement; they simply show their need for clarification.

"I'm not questioning authority," an immigrant says, "but why do I have to attend three out of four meetings? I'm already a public school teacher with ten years of experience. I also have a Bible college diploma. So why do I have to come?"

If native leaders get offended, they've missed the point. A response that will make sense to immigrants is: "We have requirements that every person—without exception—must meet so that we know they're qualified. We want no one to slip in just because of their background."

22. Immigrants stress effectiveness and measurable benchmarks. Natives may state their goals as "We want to reach our world for Jesus." Immigrants are more specific. They say, "We will try to reach people within a one-mile radius of our church. Our goal is to see one hundred people receive the Lord as their Savior. We want to see thirty-five people go through our discipleship program." They have definite benchmarks so that at the end of the year or planning cycle they can check their progress. Either they made their goals or they didn't.

They won't be able to say, as natives have in the past, "We haven't gained any, but we haven't lost any either. We're still holding the fort; we're faithful. God is blessing our faithfulness." If the native church loses members, their ready answer is, "God is purifying and culling us. He's getting us ready for something new." Those aren't satisfactory responses to immigrants.

23. Family time is a premium consideration. Natives stopped work on Friday and had the weekend to themselves. This is no longer true, and immigrants are tied up on Saturday with a variety of activities. They seek ways to get their spirituality—but not at the expense of further dividing family time. Native leaders bragged about the activity level at the church. Immigrants are asking, "How can we coordinate all these activities?"

In native thinking, a church was successful if the pastor could brag, "We have something going on all the time. On Monday night we have men's Bible study, Tuesday night we have women's Bible study, Wednesday night we have family Bible study, Thursday we have youth group, Friday we have evangelism," and their list went on.

No more. Family needs are now making parents ask, "How can we coordinate things? If we want to go to midweek activities, can we all go Friday night? The kids can go to their place, my wife can go to the ladies' place, I can go to the men's place, and then we can get back together for twenty minutes of celebration and be on our way."

24. Pastoral care has higher demands. The needs of dysfunctional people and families will cause congregations to "out-source" pastoral care. They will have to bring in chaplains who do nothing but hospital care or counseling. Churches may choose to do out-sourcing not necessarily with someone who has no connection with the church, but with someone from whom they can cut away and say, "That is them; this is us."

25. Future churches recognize and respond to single-parent homes. At least ten million single mothers live in America. Churches need to minister to them as well as to those who have never married and those who are widowed or divorced. Churches are rethinking traditional couples' dinners and Valentine's dates. What used to be the fifth wheel will become the majority in some churches.

26. The number of younger retirees continues to grow. People are retiring at an earlier age, and they have extra time and talent for involvement, not just in the church, but also in the community.

27. America is getting grayer. If the American Association of Retired Persons became a nation, it would be the thirtieth largest nation in the world, slightly smaller in population than Argentina.

The churches in the North are losing older members, so what do you do without them? They are the ones who kept the doors open. On the other hand, the influx of people in Florida and Arizona and places in the Sunbelt makes church leaders there ask, "What do we do with them?"

Churches are struggling with how to tap into the volunteer base among the elderly who are financially stable. Many of them are healthy, and they have accumulated wisdom and have more free time than any other group. Most of all, seniors want to make the last years count.

I know of at least ten growing churches that are building senior citizen apartments right on the church complexes. Those leaders see the future and are preparing for it now— right on the church property.

28. We have the mall motif—everything under one roof. Fast-growing mega-churches have their own bookstores, gyms, weight rooms, cafeterias, and childcare facilities. This means that futuring churches are becoming more entrepreneurial. The bookstore may be run by someone outside the church. The church is following the mall concept. The big anchor stores don't own their buildings; they lease them from the mall developer. This is increasingly the mind-set of growing churches.

I've been in churches that have so many international members that they sell products from the countries represented—headgear, handbags, shirts, dresses, and novelty items. Why not sell them? The church benefits, and individuals do too.

29. Multimedia will be an increasing reality. Because immigrants are visual learners, future church leaders increasingly use visual forms of communication. At our church when the pastor preaches, his main points are scrolling on a screen right above him.

30. Technology—e-mail, connecting people—will have major implications for how we do ministry, especially in global missions. Mail used to take weeks to get to other countries, but with e-mail we can communicate in real time and take immediate actions. Services such as UPS, FedEx, and DHL have speeded up the world. They specialize in overseas mail and guarantee that any size package will reach its destination within three days.

31. Consumerism has come to church. Future-oriented churches are providing leadership, education, diet, exercise, and a lot of other things. People can buy Christian exercise videos, books or tapes of Christian business principles, and self-help books. Congregations will learn to do packaging to reach out to consumers and to resource them. For instance, the pastor of a growing church will have tapes and books and resources available for the people.

32. Money is now plentiful. There's an unprecedented transfer of wealth. The bottom line is this: Trillions of dollars are going to be flowing from one generation down to the next, and that generation is fairly well set themselves. The giving generation is now saying, "I want to leave my estate in a legacy that will be worthwhile rather than fund somebody's lifestyle."

Philanthropy has taken on huge roles. How success is measured has changed. A growing number of Christian philanthropists measure success by the amount of money given away.

33. Financial accountability is a must. Immigrants are not interested in micromanaging, but they want to see the larger picture. Future churches regularly publish one-page financial statements or broad categories of income and expenses that provide the information immigrants want to know.

34. Urbanization or cross-cultural shifts are becoming the rule. By the year 2025, more than 38 percent of Americans will be ethnic minorities, and Hispanics will be the largest minority. Urbanization means that the trend of moving to the suburbs will shift as people move back into the cities. This movement will throw people into a cross-cultural world, so church leaders need to understand the variety of cultures that will become the mainstay of churches and businesses.

35. The concept of missions is changing. No longer is the church thinking of missions only as work in foreign lands; now they're including urban areas and inner cities. International missionaries are focusing on the United States. Furthermore, the church is moving toward short-term rather than long-term missions. In the old days, missionaries served four years with a fifth year of furlough.

Another change is that instead of being sending agencies, churches are becoming going agencies. More and more churches are going churches rather than sending churches.

Even if missionaries stay in a foreign country for a year, they're not out of contact with the home church. When they return, they don't have to spend a year doing what we used to refer to as deputation work, raising funds to return. Those with denominational support haven't always had that pressure, of course. Even so, the trend is still to raise total support for a family or individual within the congregation.

36. Social action is receiving a strong emphasis—especially partnership with government programs. Because of collaborative government funding, there is an explosion of nonprofit organizations. The federal government won't give money to a church, but they will give to other types of non-profit groups, so some churches are incorporating as nonprofit under a different name with a separate board. Corporations are also more open to funding such nonprofit groups.

Social action is done in partnership with government programs. The 501(c)3 nonprofit organizations are exploding around us because there is more collaborative government money available through the Department of Housing and Urban Development (HUD), the Department of Education, and especially through the rehab sections of our city governments. The issue of separation of church and state doesn't even come into play when HUD gives money to a nonprofit group because they're serving the homeless. It's the same ministry your church would have been doing, but now the government is funding it.

37. Futuring churches are increasingly active in local politics. Churches can't endorse candidates; however, people from within the church are being encouraged to run for school boards and county commissions with the unofficial support of their church. Christians involved in politics hold their meetings off church property. Increasingly, futuring congregations are saying, "We will not take a backseat and leave the driving up to others. We will help put our own people in the driver's seat."

For immigrants, politics has been redefined as a process through which community values are implemented. Politics used to be a bad word. Pastors would say, "We don't have politics in our church." What they didn't recognize is that we have politics in our churches, our homes, and our workplaces—wherever people are involved. Immigrants are saying, "Because this is the case, let's see how this works, get into the process, and make a positive contribution."

38. Church and state issues change. In 1998 former Senator John Ashcroft sponsored a bill called Charitable Choice that gave corporations permission to donate money to faith-based institutions and receive tax deductions on those gifts.

The White House, under the direction of George W. Bush, set up a division called Faith-Based Community Initiatives. Now future-facing churches can compete for and receive money for faith-based childcare centers, rehab centers, hospice centers, subsidized housing, and other projects.

39. Shared church facilities will increase. More churches are constructing multipurpose buildings in which they set up chairs on Sunday for worship and play volleyball and basketball on Monday and Wednesday. Other churches with traditional buildings are sharing the facilities with Christian groups. I foresee that two or more congregations will jointly own facilities. Churches are also building auditoriums separate from the church and renting the space for such things as banquets and weddings. As long as they report it as unrelated income, the IRS allows it.

40. The doctrine of tolerance remains an immense challenge to the health of the church. Christians want to be inclusive and not hurt others, but unless we're especially cautious, the lines will continue to blur and the Christian edges will become soft.

I see this as the greatest challenge to the health of the church. How do we become so inclusive that we don't hurt anyone and yet draw the line on behavior and practices that are contrary to our beliefs? For instance, how do we continue to stress the love of God for everyone, accept Muslims and Hindus as people loved by God, and yet draw the line?

Some churches have become so tolerant that they are saying, in effect, it doesn't matter what people believe. This is the great danger we face, because we're then apt to believe anything. As Christians, at some point we have to say, "This is what we believe. This is the core of our faith. You don't have to believe as we do, but don't try to make us embrace your faith."

41. The church is suffering and will suffer persecution. More people were martyred in the twentieth century than in the rest of the centuries combined, especially in countries such as the Sudan, China, Pakistan, and India. The church has always thrived under persecution, and that's when purification takes place.

Persecution in the United States will be more subtle. Groups such as the American Civil Liberties Union blatantly oppose the church, but we will see more subtle forms in the workplace and with individuals, especially because we believe Jesus provides the only way to God. An accusation of intolerance may well be the most powerful weapon raised against Christians.

42. Cult activity and satanic powers continue to have a great influence on our world. Multiculturalism also brings pluralism, and that opens the doors to every religion. Twenty years ago, who would have believed that a city in the Deep South would have Hindu temples and Muslim mosques?

Other gods are coming to America via people from a higher economic level than the average factory worker. More than half of the 35,000 East Indians who live in Atlanta are professionals who have power, organization, and money.

The church has two ways to approach this situation. The first is to become an apologetic congregation—in the true sense of the word. That doesn't mean we need to apologize for our stance, but that we know what we believe and defend or speak up for it. The second approach is to educate Christians to know the reality of the faith, to teach them so that they are fully grounded in the faith. They may not know how to answer every argument raised by Muslims, but they can become so familiar with the real that the counterfeit will not feel right. When the kind and highly educated neighbor who lives in a beautiful house and drives a Mercedes Benz tries to introduce them to a new way of thinking, they will be able to discern that it is wrong.

Perhaps an illustration will help. In the old days, when banks trained tellers to deal with cash, one of the final areas of their training was the vault. For hours they did nothing but feel money. The idea was that their fingers would become so sensitive that they would know a counterfeit when they touched it. Likewise, futuring churches have to train their members to detect counterfeit religions. We have to be more biblically-based in teaching the fundamentals of the truth so that our members can easily detect the counterfeit.

43. Both false prophets and true prophets are emerging. Anybody who has money can buy airtime, so we'll see a mixture of false and true prophets on TV. Web sites also are leading people down strange paths. The worst false prophets will be those who are close to the truth and say enough of the right words so that they are seductive and lead many astray.

44. Future churches live and flourish with contradictions. Traditions of the past are now being pushed aside, and there is no longer just one right way to do things. This touches everything from music to social activities. Living with contradictions will increasingly become a part of who we are and what we do. Futuring leaders and their congregations are willing to embrace contradictions and live at peace.

I present these forty-four trends as catalysts to challenge future thinking. My biggest concern is that natives continue to broadcast on AM and immigrants have tuned in to FM. Nothing is wrong with either of their receivers. But no matter how good the receiver, we don't get both frequencies at the same time. The AM stations are crying out, "If only people were more committed," while the FM stations are saying, "How will this bring meaning to me?" In this chapter I've tried to point out the issues that futuring leaders and all Christian congregations are facing or will face in the near future. Now let's look at the kind of leadership we need to go boldly into that looming future.

FIFTEEN

FIVE MAJOR APPEALS

JUST BECAUSE WE MAY BE MOTIVATED does not mean others will sense or feel the same inspiration. In fact, I constantly hear wailing statements such as: "If only people were more committed." "If only they would rise to the challenge."

Duty as a motivating fuel has lost its effectiveness. Therefore, I want to suggest that there are five motivational fuels for the flourishing twenty-first-century church and then conclude with the ones that are the most effective. First we need to pause and ask: Which of these appeals would energize God's people in this century? What frequency are we broadcasting on? What frequency are the people in our church tuned in to?

1. Compassion. Compassion is other-centered. It describes sharing with one another, serving and caring for others, giving to others, and behaving lovingly toward others.

2. Community. This is where we have our roots, our place of belonging. Even in our fragmented world, people want to belong more now than ever before. People find community in country clubs, hunting clubs, churches, and volunteer and civic organizations, because all of us want and need to belong. Community also includes relationships with family and friends.

3. Challenge. We urge others to attain more, to accomplish more, and to achieve more with their lives.

4. Reasonability. We appeal to data, logic, analysis, and good sense.

5. Commitment. We appeal to loyalty, duty, obligation, or vows.

Of these five motivational fuels leaders use, I believe that churches that stress compassion and community will thrive the best in the coming years. Why not the others? Let's examine them.

Challenge. When people come to our church, we fail to realize that they've been challenged all week long to obtain more, accomplish more, and achieve more. They don't want to be pushed, and they are seeking something different. If they go to a church where challenge is the motivating fuel, that's just like another day of the week for them.

Reasonability. Although reasonability sounds good, again that's what people are involved with all day long, every day of the work week. They're overwhelmed with data, logic, analysis, and good sense whether they're salespeople, CEOs, or schoolteachers. When they come to a place of worship, why would they want the same appeal?

Commitment. We make a serious mistake when we plead for commitment too soon. We know that just because they sign a pledge card doesn't mean they're committed. Commitment is an issue of the heart, and, therefore, appealing to commitment scares people away rather than invites them in.

This leaves us with two inviting, motivating fuels: compassion and community.

Compassion refers to connecting at a "soul level," and our motivation is beyond reciprocity and self-indulgence. It is other-focused. At the end of our lives, we then recognize meaningful fulfillment at a deeper level than if we had just done many good deeds.

Compassion involves five qualities: sharing, caring, giving, loving, and serving.

Community is about connections with an emphasis on commonality. Our individualistic society has driven us back to the beginnings of God's plan for the human race. We were created as gregarious community dwellers. Our deepest need is to be with others and to weave a common bond. Our penal system, for example, shows this clearly. Aside from execution, the harshest punishment is for a prisoner to be placed in solitary confinement.

People today want to feel that they are a vital part of a group; that is, they want to experience community. For at least a century we've pushed for individuality.

Now we're realizing that that has led to a hunger to be part of a group or organization.

In corporations, almost everyone works in cubicles. So where do they meet for community? Many businesses have an unofficial hangout where employees go after work to wind down before they go home and to reconnect with human beings after sitting in front of machines all day.

Although we live in an individualistic society, our need to connect strongly pulls us into community. The church has a great opportunity to reach out and meet that need.

SIXTEEN

LIVING IN EPIC TIMES

WE LIVE IN EPIC TIMES. This is an acrostic.

Experiential says, "We've talked enough. Stop talking and just do it."

Participatory says, "Count me in. I want to participate in this."

Icon-driven says, "You have to draw the picture for me. Let me see it for myself."

Connection says, "That connects with me. I want to belong."

The best way I can illustrate that is to point to the amazing success of eBay, Inc., without advertising. This company describes itself as one that "provides person-to-person trading community on the Internet where buyers and sellers are brought together." eBay is worth more than many of the anchor chain stores at our malls. They are successful because they understand the times.

Those of us trained in the last century were trained with words. We put emphasis on what we said and how we said it. Today people learn with pictures. Preachers and teachers who paint with words are master communicators. We can take listeners where we want them to go if they can "see" what we mean.

In the final chapter I point out the five challenges futuring leaders in all areas of the church face.

SEVENTEEN

NEW LEADERSHIP STYLES

L IKE ALL FAITHFUL JEWS, JOSEPH and Mary took their twelve-year-old son, Jesus, to the Passover feast in Jerusalem (see Luke 2:41–52). This wasn't their first trip; in fact, it was a trip they took every year to follow the Old Testament law. Thus, it was a tradition—the way they did things. Tradition isn't bad, but for some people, repetitiveness finally loses its meaning.

I'm going to spiritualize this story—that is, I'm going to speak of events and people as symbolic. I'm quite aware that was not Luke's intent in writing the story; but by spiritualizing it, I can use it to show the native versus immigrant mentality more clearly.

Joseph and Mary represent the old church, or the natives. Jesus represents the immigrants, or the new church. In this well-known story, after the feast, Jesus' parents leave and assume Jesus is with them. While his parents start their return to Nazareth to live as usual, Jesus stays in Jerusalem. He's there beginning to fulfill his calling.

For three days, Mary and Joseph do not even know that Jesus is not with them, which is a way of saying that many of our churches don't even know that they've stopped being effective. They're still doing what they were doing; for them, it's business as usual. They may have started out exciting and innovative, but they don't realize that they have lost the cutting edge.

What happens when Mary and Joseph discover the boy is gone? They do the obvious—they search for him among the familiar, among relatives and friends, but Jesus isn't there. They do some serious thinking and return to the place where they last saw their son. This is like going back to where the church lost its cutting edge. They finally find him and are shocked at their discovery.

Four things are going on in verses 46 and 47:

1. Jesus listens to the traditional leaders—the priests and teachers.

2. Jesus asks questions.

3. Jesus understands their answers.

4. Jesus gives them answers.

Notice that Jesus did three things before he gave answers. That's characteristic of effective futuring leaders.

First, if you are going to be such a leader, you need to listen. Listen to what people—especially the people in your congregation—are saying.

Second, after you've heard, ask questions for clarification. Stay at it until you've asked all the relevant questions. Third, ponder their responses and understand the issues and needs. Don't be in a hurry to solve issues or give great advice. Don't do anything until you're sure you understand the complexity of the situation.

Finally, you're prepared to give answers—but only after you have gone through the first three steps.

Jesus' parents return to the place where they left their son. They retrace their steps. As soon as Mary sees Jesus, she asks, "Why are you treating us this way?" She's asking the "us versus them" question. Why are you treating us this way?

This is the point of tension between the natives and the immigrants. Jesus doesn't really answer, but he points out that he must be about the Father's business. In the traditional church, there is tension between the business of the church and the business of the kingdom.

The immigrant is more kingdom oriented while the natives are still locked into the traditions of the past.

Mary and Joseph merely shook their heads. They didn't get it. How could this kid know so much and be so bright? They were older and had been part of the Jewish system all their lives, yet he was showing them up. That's a way to say that if futuring leaders expect the natives to understand immigrant thinking, they can forget it. Too often it is impossible for natives to make that mental adjustment. Futuring leaders have learned to live with this tension between the two groups. It's also true that most of the time the immigrants won't understand the natives.

The hopeful note in this story is the way it ends. "Then [Jesus] returned to Nazareth with them and was obedient to them; and his mother stored all these things in her heart" (Luke 2:51 NLT). An older translation says that she "pondered these things." Mary, the native, didn't just ignore or deny what she heard. Later, when Jesus had completed his ministry and died on the cross, his mother was there. Somehow the native had learned to think like an immigrant.

Finally, I want to conclude by giving church leaders five suggestions for becoming more effective futurefaith leaders.

1. Focus the majority of your efforts on the future. Even though I exhort leaders to think of the future, I'm aware that most of their followers are bogged down in the present. They're coping with getting their children to soccer practice on time, paying off their credit card balances, recovering from divorce, or worrying about putting a parent in a nursing facility. Effective leaders acknowledge this and try to be available to help in any way possible. While they wrap arms around the dazed or hurting, they also keep a large portion of their attention fixed on the future. They need to see the crises that are still too far ahead for problem-plagued members to grapple with.

They need to foresee the problems—and opportunities—that will face the congregation in a few weeks or months. If they are properly focused, drastic changes won't take them by surprise, and they'll have their people prepared to cope with them.

2. Understand the fundamental nature of change. New paradigms show up before we need them, and they take the unprepared by surprise. Stay in touch with the outside world, and don't allow yourself to be confined to your congregation or your denomination. Most of the time, those who are not part of the present system introduce changes. Too many insiders accept life as it is and often push away anything that demands change.

You, as the leader, need to understand the fundamental nature of change. Ask yourself, "What is change, and how do I bring about change?" If you're a futuring leader, you'll make change a major part of your study. You have to become a specialist in the area of change or your leadership just won't be effective in this century.

3. Appreciate complex systems and how they work. How does your church fit into the community? How does the community fit into your city? How does the city fit into the county? How does all of that come back to your church? How do the people in your church interweave their lives with you and your staff? When a family goes through troubled times, how does that bear on the way your church functions? Once we understand complex systems and how they interrelate, we can become effectively involved in the systems and in change.

4. Examine your leadership style. Too few church leaders pause to think carefully about their leadership style. Often they assume there is only one way to lead and don't question whether they might learn a better style.

I suggest you start with several questions:

- What is my delegation style?
- Do I dump or do I delegate?
- Do I give authority and then yank it back?
- Do I need to be in control of every situation?

You are a leader, and I have never met a strong leader who didn't have some problems with control. That's probably one reason you are a leader! The downside is it goes back to the lid or the ceiling of the helium-filled balloon. That's the ceiling on your productivity.

Here are more self-study questions:

- Do you manage your time well?
- Are you organized or haphazard?
- Do you start each day with a sense of what you need to accomplish next?

5. Create a shared vision to build bridges to the future. The emphasis here is on shared vision. In the church, people need your vision, but they also want a voice in their future. Effective futuring leaders build bridges and encourage others to join them on the journey across the bridge. Shared visions mean, "It isn't my vision; it's our vision."

CONCLUSION

Someone once said, "Everything we see today came about because someone first thought about it." That's obvious, but many of us tend to forget what goes on before the action.

Thinking, conceptualizing, and planning must come first. I've observed many leaders who become highly excited over activity (visible) but have little regard for transformational thinking (invisible).

They quickly engage in "making things happen" instead of standing back and considering the process and the effects of their action in the months and years ahead.

One primary purpose of this book is to underscore the need for atypical ways of thinking that lead to different conclusions and thus envision new strategies. Thus, futuring calls us to contextualize leadership and view it as a process rather than a set of activities.

As we move into tomorrow with our leadership, here are two things we need to keep before us:

1. Leadership tasks are never finished. As change agents, we remain part of the process.

2. Our thoughts and processes display integrity only if our lifestyle is congruous with those thoughts and processes. This means that it's not what we do as much as who we are. We shift the emphasis from doing to being. Just as leaders enter a different level of leadership when they move from projects (what) to people (who).

Futuring: Leading Your Church into Tomorrow invites you to take this exciting journey where the little creature from the film *ET* can't take you—but God can.

CPSIA information can be obtained
at www.ICGtesting.com
Printed in the USA
FFOW05n1546230517